Diana **K**rall

The Language of Love

Diana **K**rall

The Language of Love

Jamie Reid

QUARRY
MUSIC
BOOKS

The publisher acknowledges the support of the Government of
Canada, Department of Canadian Heritage, Book Publishing
Industry Development Program.

Diana Krall: The Language of Love is a serious critical and
biographical study of the music and career of this artist. The
quotation of lyrics from songs written or performed by Diana
Krall illustrates the biographical and critical analysis presented
by the author and thus constitutes fair use under existing copy-
right conventions. The authors of all lyrics cited in the text are
duly credited.

ISBN 1-55082-297-7
Library of Congress and National Library of Canada
cataloguing information is available.

Design by Gordon Robertson.
Typeset by Susan Hannah.

Printed and bound in Canada by Transcontinental,
Peterborough, Ontario.

Published by Quarry Press Inc., 195 Allstate Parkway,
Markham, Ontario, Canada L3R 4T8.

Contents

A Canadian in **P**aris

Tonight Canadian jazz pianist and vocalist Diana Krall is appearing at the Olympia Theatre in Paris, accompanied not only by her usual trio, but also, for this special occasion, by the Orchestre Symphonie Europeen and the Paris Jazz Big Band, a performance that is being taped for delayed television broadcast under the marquee, *Diana Krall in Paris*. Diana Krall is far from the first jazz musician to appear on the Olympia's famed stage. Louis Armstrong, canonized by Ken Burns as the inventor of jazz, played to full houses, as did Django Reinhardt, master jazz guitarist, Alberta Hunter, the sweetest of all early jazz singers, and Ella Fitzgerald, the first lady of jazz. Armstrong found a haven in Paris when he fled from America to escape a marijuana charge in the 1930s and returned to the Olympia stage triumphantly in the 1960s. Reinhardt and his Hot Five Club band, featuring Belgian violin virtuoso Stephane Grapelli, revolutionized jazz instrumentation when he merged the music of two oppressed minorities, the Afro-American and the European gypsy. Alberta Hunter was embraced by sophisticated Parisienne audiences at a time when her music found little favor in America. And the greatest of all female jazz singers, Ella Fitzgerald, sang songs like Ira and George Gershwin's *'S Wonderful* from the soundtrack of *An American in*

Paris on this stage to rapt audiences. The love affair of the City of Lights with that North American music known as jazz continues to this day.

Of all the places where jazz has been played in Paris, the Olympia Theatre at 29 rue des Capucins is the most famous, a staging ground for modern music of every kind from every country. The Olympia is to Paris what Albert Hall is to London or Carnegie Hall is to New York. First built in 1888, the Theatre was refurbished in 1954, and then again in 1997. The list of musicians who have appeared on this stage reads like an encyclopedia of modern jazz and popular music. The Olympia has been the home of the most adored of all French chanteuses, the divine Edith Piaf, and the great French songwriter, Jacques Brel. Americans who have appeared here are equally legendary in jazz and pop circles — Judy Garland, Count Basie, Stan Getz, the Modern Jazz Quartet, Frank Sinatra, Miles Davis, Dionne Warwick, Thelonious Monk, Art Blakey and his Jazz Messengers, John Coltrane, Donald Byrd, Aretha Franklin, Eric Dolphy, Ahmad Jamal, Ike and Tina Turner, Jimi Hendrix, James Brown, Deep Purple, Paul Simon, Harry Connick Jr. The Beatles performed here in 1964, months before they became international celebrities with their appearance on the *Ed Sullivan Show*.

On this hallowed stage, a cool, blond, and beautiful woman appears, undoubtedly the first Canadian female jazz pianist and singer ever to appear here in a headline role. A white, female, jazz artist on the stage of the Olympia Theatre in Paris? And this singer is from *where*? From Nanaimo, British Columbia, Canada? A town so distant from the cosmopolitan cities where jazz is usually played that it is not even on the mainland of the continent, a town located off the North American coast, on an island.

The appearance of Diana Krall on the Olympia stage is all the more extraordinary for the fact that her celebrity has been so astonishingly sudden, taking everyone totally by surprise, including herself, her producers, and the entire world of popular music. Six years ago, she was virtually unknown outside of a few aficionados in the local jazz scenes in New York, Toronto, Los

Angeles, and Vancouver. Her first album, the aptly titled STEP-
PING OUT, was not released until 1993 when she was already
nearly 30 years old. Throughout the late 1980s and early 1990s
she played in small hotel lounges and piano bars. "When I'd show
up," Diana recalled in a *Time* magazine feature with David E.
Thigpen, "they'd ask, 'Where's the piano player?' I'd say, 'I am
the piano player!'"

Diana opens her Olympia show by performing one of the jazz
standards she has made her own, *I Love Being Here With You*, from
her second album, ONLY TRUST YOUR HEART. As she adds her individual talent to this tradition, she pays homage to Ella and Count
Basie, just as Peggy Lee and Nat King Cole had done before.

> I love the East, I love the West
> North and South, they're both the best
> But I only want to go there as a guest
> 'Cause I love being here with you . . .
>
> I love good wine, fine cuisine
> Candlelight I love the scene
> 'Cause baby if you know what I mean
> I love being here with you
>
> I love Ella singing, Basie's band is swinging
> 'Cause that's something else you know
> They know how to play it, they know how to say it
> They just wind it up and let it go . . .
>
> I love being here with you
> — PEGGY LEE/BILL SCHLUGER

The success of her next album, ALL FOR YOU, a tribute to Nat
King Cole, along with a landmark performance at the Montreal
Jazz Festival and her first Grammy Award nomination, brought
Diana Krall her first small measure of celebrity. This was fol-
lowed in 1997 by the phenomenal success of her fourth album,

LOVE SCENES, which won her a second Grammy nomination and became one of the most commercially successful jazz albums of all time. Selling more than 500,000 units, LOVE SCENES was certified Gold by RIAA on August 12, 1999. Her fifth album, WHEN I LOOK IN YOUR EYES, featured the orchestral stylings of no less a jazz figure than Johnny Mandel surrounding her trio. Released on June 6, 1999, this work was the first jazz recording in 25 years to receive a Grammy Award nomination for Best Album. When the album actually won a Grammy for Best Jazz Vocal in 2000, Diana was catapulted into international jazz superstardom. THE LOOK OF LOVE, released in September 2001 and featuring arrangements by Claus Ogerman played by the London Symphony Orchestra and the Los Angeles session orchestra, has already gone platinum. In the television listings of record sales on the Bravo arts and entertainment channel, THE LOOK OF LOVE was number one for several weeks, outselling the celebrated re-release of Miles Davis' KIND OF BLUE and the Louis Armstrong CD from Ken Burns' landmark *Jazz* documentary.

There have been many other honors along the way: a tour with Tony Bennett and a duet with this master singer on a recent album of blues songs; a duet with the redoubtable Rosemary Clooney; appearances at Carnegie Hall in tributes to jazz giants Ella Fitzgerald and Benny Carter; an appearance with Erykah Badu and George Benson at the Grammy Awards celebrations in 2001; two separate appearances at President Bill Clinton's White House, one of them a state dinner for Canadian Prime Minister Jean Chretien and his wife Aline.

When the *Diana Krall in Paris* special is broadcast, the show opens with an image of a rain-soaked Paris street. Reflected in reverse in the shimmering liquid are the simple words, "Diana Krall in Paris." In the background, the neon-lit façade of the Olympia Theatre appears while Diana and her trio play a brisk up-tempo number, the bright notes of the piano framed in a smooth guitar and bass accompaniment, restrained percussion on the drums and cymbals. The street scene gives way to an image of the stage with a close up of Diana as she pumps the keys over the black piano case. She seems barely aware of the presence of the camera or the audience, engrossed in the sounds her fingers are drawing from the keyboard and the sounds of her accompanists behind her. She sings for a while, a quick, boppy, scat-like vocal — scat-like, but all the words succinctly pronounced. Then she stops singing but continues to play the piano, sometimes shaking her head and pursing her lips in response to the sounds her own fingers are producing from the piano. She is relaxed; she's at ease. There is no sense of worry or pressure in her playing. She seems apart from the audience in some important way, not lost in the music, but fully concentrating in her calm and determined way on making the music right. This concentration is the only compliment she pays to the audience, her modest effort to make the music the best that she and her band of musicians can make it. This serene modesty towards her own singing abilities and this quiet confidence in her playing creates a charismatic presence.

On stage in the act of playing, Diana Krall is even more beautiful than in the glamorous photographs gracing her recent album covers. On these lavish (some say, over-lavish) album covers, she appears in elegant couturier fashions—watery silk, glistening moires, blue or shimmering cerise, expensive and luxurious pearlescent silk. But on stage at the Olympia, she is very simply dressed — an elegant jacket, ribbed at the shoulders, made of leather so fine and so well-crafted that it looks as light as fabric, zippered to the neck. In between musical phrases, her long-fingered hands sweep her long and silky blond hair back from her face. She is almost without make-up — with only a hint of pale lipstick on her full and sensuous lips. She looks for all the world as if she has just come on stage from washing her face, her transparent complexion youthful and dewy, fresh as an adolescent's. Her teeth are as white and straight as the keys on her Steinway grand. She has all the beauty, poise, and allure of a ravishing star of the silver screen, a Veronica Lake or a Lauren Bacall, and all their mysterious cool reserve.

The first two tunes, *I Love Being Here With You* and *'Deed I Do*, are played cleverly and swingingly in rapid tempos with breakneck vocals. After a break for commercials, a CBC announcer introduces Diana in typical Canadian fashion, modestly, anonymously, without any sign of fanfare or inflation for the sake of publicity. He remarks that Diana's appearance at the Olympia signals her arrival as the latest international jazz superstar, fully competent to appear on the same stage as Louis, Ella, and Edith Piaf. Then Diana returns to the screen. She does not announce the names of the tunes she plays and sings. She lets the words of the songs speak for themselves. Most of the tunes are so well known they require no introduction anyway. Diana's singing diction is so precise that the title of each song is immediately recognizable.

She whistles through a repertoire of tunes mainly drawn from her best-selling new album, THE LOOK OF LOVE. Who needs to be told that she is singing *Devil May Care* by Bob Dorough, *Cry Me A River* by Julie London, *I've Got You Under My Skin* by Cole Porter, *Pick Yourself Up* by Jerome Kern and Dorothy Fields, *'S Wonderful* by Ira and George Gershwin, or *The Look Of Love* by Burt Bacharach and Hal David? The words say it all.

> The look of love is in your eyes
> A look your smile can't disguise
> The look of love, it's saying so much more
> Than these words could ever say . . .
>
> I can hardly wait to hold you
> Feel my arms around you
> Now that I have found you
> Don't ever go
> Don't ever go
> I love you so
>
> — BURT BACHARACH AND HAL DAVID

Once a hit for the great pop singer Dusty Springfield, Diana Krall transforms this song into a jazz classic. These songs have been done and done again by all of the masters of American popular music and jazz — Frank Sinatra, Nat King Cole, Peggy

Lee, Rosemary Clooney, Ella Fitzgerald, Billy Holiday, Barbra Streisand. Echoes of the influence of all of these singers can be heard in Diana's artful phrasing and melody-making, even though her own voice and presentation belong to no one else.

Other Paris scenes are superimposed on the stage as she plays: a boulevard lined by trees in autumn, its empty benches strewn with leaves, a panning shot of the wet stones of a walkway by the Seine. Against these images appears the ghostly image of Diana's hands caressing the piano keys, their reflection on the piano case. Images follow of the inner workings of the piano, gold-tipped wooden rectangular hammers lifting and falling on the piano strings, shots of the orchestra, leaning intently into their scores, one or two of them occasionally glancing over their instruments toward the lead performer.

Diana's usual guitar accompanist, Russell Malone, is missing, along with his uncanny telepathic ability, heard on most of her records, to respond to the varied moods that Diana sketches with her voice and piano. His place is taken by Anthony Wilson, whose smiling demeanor seems to be out of place with his fabulous skill on the guitar. He flawlessly plays one delicate and lengthy guitar run after another, winning nods of approval from Diana and several rounds of applause and shouts of approval from the audience.

There, too, is John Clayton, like Diana, once also a protégé of Ray Brown, playing the stand-up bass. The calm intelligent face of this director of the Hollywood Bowl jazz orchestra is wreathed with proud smiles. Jeff Hamilton, surely one of the smoothest of all jazz drummers, robust and red-bearded, plays a stream of melodic brush work. These two musicians have played alongside Diana for years; they, too, play with confidence and style, understanding the nuances of her singing and playing, showcased in her rendition of a song Julie London made famous, *Cry Me A River*:

Now you say you're lonely
You cry the long night through
Well, cry me a river

Cry me a river
I cried a river over you . . .

   – ARTHUR HAMILTON

Throughout the performance, Diana smiles rarely, and then only to nod an acknowledgement to Anthony Wilson. The music is delivered straight, no chaser, without the least excess, no expansive or showy gestures. There is the barest hint of drama, just a touch of performance art, restrained and minimal. Her presence, slightly dreamy, in the mood of the music, never distracts from the music itself. Diana Krall seems to eschew the dramatic postures favored by most singers, the smiles and facial expressions meant to convince the audience of the singer's commitment to the emotion of the song. Her own concentration has the effect of focusing the listener's concentration directly on the music.

There are some jazz critics who still claim that Diana's celebrity is the result of 'production values' inflating a talent which otherwise might never command so much attention. Yet if this Olympia performance was a production for a well-known rock and roll band or for any of the other music divas of Diana Krall's generation — Whitney Houston, for example, or Mariah Carey, or Celine Dion, not to speak of Britney Spears — there would be expensive special effects, fire works, sparkling lights, fog and smoke, dancers, extravagant gowns and costumes. In our culture of excess, these production values have become the expected complement to any kind of musical performance, but not in this case. There are no fireworks, no special lighting, no athletic displays, no flashy dancers. No displays of vocal pyrotechnics, either. Everything is simple, cool, completely restrained. Every atom of fanfare has been eliminated. The most expensive item on stage is the orchestra itself, their instruments, and, of course, the piano. Far from being overproduced, the show is remarkable above all for its bald minimalism, for foregrounding the music and the music alone.

There is a sense of tremendous relief for once to view a celebrated popular musician who is present on stage only and solely to present the music, unadorned. In interview after interview, Diana Krall has asserted that her main concern is not for her own beauty or glamor, or for the publicity which the nature of the music industry forces upon her, for the celebrity she is now receiving or for anything else but the beauty of the music she plays and sings, and tries to honor in that process. She seems completely the "errand girl for rhythm" that the first song on her tribute album to Nat King Cole proclaims her to be.

> ... If you want to swing and shout
> Get your heels and get about
> I'm an errand girl for rhythm, send me
>
> Just get hip and follow through
> I'll deliver straight to you
> I'm an errand girl for rhythm, send me ...
>
> — NAT KING COLE

Her fingers, lightly relaxed, are playing intricate short runs, brisk trills. Totally practiced, totally confident, they seem never to miss or falter even over the most complicated passages. Everything is made to seem simple and easy. Every note in every one of the liquid runs is made to count, to add to the total rhythmic and sonic atmosphere.

And then there is the voice. The critics have commented on her "luxuriously supple alto," "trademark husky voice and clipped delivery," and "mischievous sense of humor," her "deft, minimalist touch on the keyboard," her "witty, theatrical way with a lyric," her "deep respect for the roots of jazz," the "husky, even dusky, timbre" of her "bluesy, mahogany-grained voice," the "arresting" quality of "her dark, hot alto, like blue smoke," "like mink draped over mahogany," her "dusky, deadpan contralto with its hairline cracks," her "empathy and intelligence," a "smooth, stainless steel quality, strong and clean, though capable of a soft refrain and even a blues tinge," and her "effortless command of phrasing and intonation." A European admirer writes about her "smoky, disreputable *sprechgesang*," referring to what some Americans have called her "conversational style" of delivering lyrics.

American critics have compared her to Peggy Lee, Ernestine Anderson, Carmen MacRae, Shirley Horn, Julie London, Abbey Lincoln, Nina Simone, singers who are lesser known, perhaps than the greatest of jazz singers like Ella Fitzgerald, Sarah Vaughan, and Billy Holiday. The British and European jazz critics are less restrained, openly declaring their enthusiasm by comparing her to the greatest, Fitzgerald and Holiday.

Her few detractors deride her music as "ingenue jazz," accusing her of putting style over substance, a product of image-making and marketing rather than real musical talent. A critic for the *Rolling Stone* has suggested that her style is solely derivative of Shirley Horn, suggesting that instead of listening to Diana's records, we should attend to the Horn originals instead. The 'jazz police', to use the term Diana borrowed from Leonard Cohen to describe her detractors, argue that Diana has achieved only a temporary celebrity, the result of marketing professionals playing upon an ignorant mass market, listeners who have no knowledge of jazz and no real love of the music, but are drawn to listen to Diana's records only on the strength of a glamorous persona. They seem to resent the idea that Diana's pre-eminence is somehow depriving other more 'genuine' jazz artists of the audience she has seized so peremptorily, without earning her credentials, without paying her proper dues.

But Diana Krall has paid her dues. She has apprenticed to the very finest jazz musicians. Her closest mentor has been none other than Ray Brown, the legendary jazz bassist who began his career with the Dizzy Gillespie Quintet and who was once the husband and manager of Ella Fitzgerald. In his notes to Diana's first album, Brown remarked on her 'beautiful phrasing" and gave her the ultimate compliment for any jazz musician when he commented on her rendition of the classic *Body And Soul*, "I find there is a lot of soul inside this lady." When Brown first 'discovered' Diana when she was 17 years old back in 1981, he opened doors in Los Angeles for her to study under jazz master pianist Jimmy Rowles. Today she plays with some of the most distinguished mainstream jazz players to be found in America. An accomplished bass player like John Clayton, a drummer like Jeff Hamilton, or her regular guitar player, Russell Malone, would not consent to act as her sidemen, without respecting her musical abilities, since their own musical taste and abilities are so surpassingly high.

Apart from the taste and restraint of Diana Krall's musical presentation, her repertoire alone sets her apart from dozens of other singers. At a very young age, as a pianist who had not yet become a singer, coming from a generation born and raised on the driving rhythms and harmonic simplicities of rock and roll, she decided that her favorite music was jazz with its greater rhythmic and musical subtlety, allowing a deeper kind of emotional expression. She chose the musical territory she wanted to inhabit and tenaciously pursued a career as a jazz pianist without any thought at that time of becoming a celebrity, striving to master the music alone, aspiring only to a decent career as a hard-working jazz instrumentalist. Her singing came almost as an afterthought, an activity she first rejected, then unwillingly took on, and finally embraced.

Today, Diana Krall is performing songs first written 20 or 30 years before she was even born, in the era before television became a mass phenomenon, before Elvis Presley, before rock and roll. These lyrics summon up stories about relationships that seem a touch dated in a contemporary context but nevertheless sound timeless in her voice, songs like the Cole Porter classic, *I Got You Under My Skin*, which she performs tonight on the Olympia stage.

> I've got you under my skin
> I've got you deep in the heart of me
> So deep in my heart
> You're nearly a part of me
> I've got you under my skin . . .
>
> I'd sacrifice anything
> Come what might

For the sake of having you near
In spite of a warning voice
That comes in the night
It repeats and it shouts in my ear

Don't you know old fool
You can never win
Use your mentality
Wake up to reality

But each time that I do
Just the thought of you
Makes me stop before I begin
'Cause I 've got you under my skin

— COLE PORTER

She follows this evocation of the 1936 movie *Born to Dance*, starring Eleanor Powell and Jimmy Stewart, with a rendition of *Pick Yourself Up* by Dorothy Fields and Jerome Lerner from the Fred Astaire and Ginger Rogers 1930s movie *Swing Time*. On the Olympia stage, Diana sings Ginger's answer to Fred's plea to teach him how to dance, "please teacher, teach me something," bringing their many cinematic love affairs back to life.

Nothing's impossible I have found
For when my chin is on the ground
I pick myself up, dust myself off
Start all over again

Don't lose your confidence if you slip
Be grateful for a pleasant trip
And pick yourself up
Dust yourself off
Start all over again

Work like a soul inspired
'Til the battle of the day is won
You may be sick and tired
But you'll be a man, my son

Will you remember the famous men
Who had to fall to rise again
So take a deep breath
Pick yourself up
Dust yourself off
Start all over again ...

    – DOROTHY FIELDS

An important part of the art of Diana Krall is her uncanny ability to recreate these songs in a manner that recalls previous versions, at the same time making these songs seem newly written, all her own.

The culture heroes who sang the songs that Diana Krall now sings, before television, before the growth of the mass market, appeared in visual form to their followers, if at all, only in short movie clips, as cameo performers in full length movies, or in still photographs in mass magazines. Adulation for pop music singers was generated differently. Today, the human voice takes second place to the image. At one time unmediated, later only slightly mediated by radio and recording, the human voice has been altered, stretched, and heightened by an array of highly sophisticated electronic devices. There is no longer any need to construct an image around a sound as there was with the old radio and record singers. In the old world of radio sound, one could live one's own life, surrounding the sound of the singer's voice with images from one's own experience, exercising one's own interior visual imagination. One could remain in possession of one's own imaginative domain. But in the world of constructed television images, one is never free to construct oneself imaginatively apart from the multifold repeated images constantly breaking into one's personal world.

Diana Krall restores sound to its proper place in music. She goes back to the voice, often the conversational voice, and to the ears that hear the voice. Of course, she has recorded videos for her songs and appeared on short sound bits on television; she has also appeared in movies and in cameo appearances on television soap operas. Just at this moment, she is appearing briefly in a commercial for an expensive American automobile. But so far, her videos have not been widely played on television. She exists in a mysterious space different from the space of the image-bound rock and roller, different from the space even of Whitney Houston, Mariah Carey, Shania Twain, Celine Dion, and others, who have relied on the video image as one of the main ways to present their 'product' to the market.

There are reasons to explain why Diana Krall has not yet become a pop icon of this stature. One of them is the fact that jazz, a sophisticated music demanding musical virtuosity from its practitioners, also demands a correspondingly high level of musical sophistication from its listeners. As such, it is a barely marketable commodity in a musical world dominated by the hype and drama of rock and roll, rap, and pop. Rock and rollers, rappers, and big-voice pop singers tend to emphasize the difficulty of their vocal feats, straining their voices, going all out, as the sign of their emotional commitment, passion, fire. Their aim seems to be to increase angst, to augment struggle and pain. Diana Krall, like the crooners of the '40s and '50s, seems to value vocal relaxation over vocal tension. The aim is to make the production of the sound seem easy, and thereby to create a relaxing atmosphere. There is artistic value in disruption, struggle, difficulty. Sometimes what is required is the screwing up of emotion to the highest level in order to find cathartic release. But there is also value in soothing emotions, in escape from tension, and in romance, love. This is what Diana Krall's healing voice delivers, along with a hidden charge of deep and intimate emotion, delivered with a tremendous range of nuance and suggestion. Intelligent reflection, deep consideration, passionate expression, a kind of poetic "emotion recollected in tranquillity"—this is what Diana Krall's music offers.

During the entire Olympia performance, Diana Krall's choice

of songs seems at every step a kind of dialog with her audience. She lets her singing and piano-playing do all her talking in her distinctive conversational style. She speaks only two times — once to introduce the members of her trio, and once again when she introduces her arranger and conductor, Claus Ogerman. For the first time, she rises from her piano bench to bring Ogerman forward to be recognized with applause from the audience. She embraces him before turning the conducting over to him for the final tune, the Ira and George Gershwin classic, *'S Wonderful.*

'S wonderful, 's marvelous
You should care for me
'S awful nice, 's paradise
'S what I love to see

You've made my life so glamorous
You can't blame me for feeling amorous
Oh 's wonderful, 's marvelous
That you should care for me

'S magnifique, 's what I seek
You should care for me
'S elegant, 's what I want
'S what I love to see …

— IRA GERSHWIN

A Canadian in Paris singing lyrics from the soundtrack for the movie *An American in Paris,* singing a song that became a signature tune for Ella Fitzgerald. The Parisienne audience loves this set of variations on a theme. Diana Krall pays tribute to their jazz sophistication. Everyone is smiling, even the piano player now.

Looking for Diana **K**rall

For weeks, I've been looking for leads to people who knew Diana Krall before she became a celebrity. The real person who once lived in Nanaimo, went to school there, played jazz in the high school band, won music scholarships in her teens, and left this small-town atmosphere at the age of 19 to move to Los Angeles, there to begin living in the jazz stratosphere. I'm looking for some stories to flesh out the basic facts, some sense of the place she comes from, the people who have been close to her, the things she did as a kid, the things she said, the way she made her way in the world as a young person. I want some color to add to the black and white record of dates and places, not only from her hometown, but from the cities that she has worked in as an adult – Vancouver, Los Angeles, Toronto, Boston, New York, and the cities of Europe where she later toured, playing with other musicians, jazz legends like Ray Brown, Jimmy Rowles, and Don Thompson.

The basic facts of her life are well known by now, widely recorded in magazines and on the internet. Diana Krall was born on November 16, 1964 in the Vancouver Island city of Nanaimo in the Canadian province of British Columbia. Her father, Jim Krall, was a chartered accountant, and her mother, Adella, an elementary school-teacher/librarian. Diana grew up in secure circumstances within a happy family. Her younger sister was born two years later. A former officer in the Royal Canadian Mounted Police in Toronto, she has moved back to Nanaimo, where she works as a publicist organizing charity events involving Diana.

Diana was enveloped in music from the very day of her birth. Her father was an avid collector of popular and classical music in all its forms — old 78s, LPs, and even old wax recording cylinders. Father and mother both played the piano and sang. Her grandmother was also a musician, and an aunt was at one time a vaudeville performer. Sunday nights, the family often met for dinner at Diana's grandmother's home, where members of the family played the piano or sang the popular songs of the day, old hymns, and Celtic folksongs — anything and everything. Diana remembers these sessions fondly; they were "like playing rummy," she has commented. Diana began to take piano lessons at the age of four from a neighbor, Audrey Thomas, and later from the well-known Victoria pianist and singer, Louise Rose. Audrey Thomas recalls that the young Diana showed a special love for the sound of boogie-woogie piano.

From all official reports, Diana's childhood and teen years were much the same as any other child growing up on Vancouver Island. She attended public schools for her elementary and secondary education. She was an athlete, a swimmer and a skier in high school, and for a time pursued a scientific interest in building and launching homemade rockets. But she showed an obvious flair for the piano that made her exceptional. By the age of fifteen, Diana was already playing professionally in two downtown Nanaimo restaurants, the NHL and Chez Michel.

During these years, a local high-school teacher and jazz bassist, Bryan Stovell, heard her playing one night on a local radio station and recognized immediately that she had a special talent. He gave her some of her first jazz albums, including the work of Bill Evans. Playing in the school band led by Stovell, Diana became more closely acquainted with the repertoire of modern jazz and continued to develop her skills. The at the age of 17, she was awarded a scholarship from a local jazz festival, which enabled her to travel to Boston to study at the prestigious Berklee College of Music until 1983.

When she returned to Nanaimo, Diana continued to play in local establishments, where she was heard one night by Ray Brown, one of the greatest players of the stand-up bass in the history of jazz, and once the husband of Ella Fitzgerald. Brown made arrangements for Diana to travel to Los Angeles, assisted by a grant from the Canada Council for the Arts, where she studied under the legendary pianist, Jimmy Rowles, widely known as a favorite accompanist to some of the greatest jazz singers of all time, including Billie Holiday and Peggy Lee. Rowles encouraged her to take up singing in addition to her piano playing. During this time, she would have played regularly with the musicians in Ray Brown's circle there — bassist John Clayton and drummer Jeff Hamilton.

In spite of her ongoing love for her hometown, Diana has stated she wanted to break out of the small-town atmosphere of Nanaimo and participate in a larger musical world. Throughout these early years, Diana believed that her voice was not strong or expressive enough to make her into a real singer. She never had any thought of pursuing a career as a singer, but she would sometimes reluctantly sing as a concession to club owners. "Just enough to keep the gig," she once said.

In 1988, she moved to Toronto, where she studied under another British Columbia native, the multi-instrumentalist, Don Thompson. She played gigs at The Underground Railroad and Meyer's Deli. She is remembered in Toronto as a dedicated musician who was often seen after hours at the Café des Copains, practicing her piano skills. Two years later in 1990, she moved to New York, commuting weekly to a gig in Boston.

Although she had begun playing with a group of some of the finest North American jazz musicians in Los Angeles at the age of 19, although she had appeared on several festival stages and had already won significant Canadian musical prizes, although her music had often been recorded and played on the Canadian Broadcasting System, and although she logged many hours of performance time, Diana Krall did not record her first album until 1992, at the age of 29, fully ten years since the beginning of her apprenticeship in Los Angeles. On this first album, mostly a collection of standards from the classic American songbook called STEPPING OUT, she was accompanied by her old Los Angeles friends, John Clayton and Jeff Hamilton. Featuring album notes written by her mentor, Ray Brown, the album was released in Canada only by Montreal's Justin Time Records.

This album led to an appearance sponsored by Justin Time at the famed Blue Note in New York, where she was heard by executives of the GRP record label. They contracted her to make a second album, ONLY TRUST YOUR HEART, which appeared the following year. On this record, Diana was accompanied by Ray Brown, drummer Lewis Nash, and beloved saxophonist Stanley Turrentine. In retrospect, Diana has stated that her vocal performances on these albums were not just "painful" but actually "torturous," recognizing her efforts to master the difficult art of vocal jazz.

Diana's third album, ALL FOR YOU, is a collection of tunes selected from the recordings of Nat King Cole as a tribute to one of her jazz idols. The album was successful, selling 250,000 copies in a single year and winning Diana her first Grammy Award nomination. With this recording her international career was launched. Each successive album — LOVE SCENES, WHEN I LOOK IN YOUR EYES, and THE LOOK OF LOVE — has been even more successful. In the course of six short years, Diana Krall has sold more albums than any other jazz musician in recent memory, and has been accorded more critical attention, both positive and negative, than any other singer currently active in jazz. Each of these new records in turn has been nominated for the coveted Grammy Award. In 2001, her album WHEN I LOOK IN YOUR EYES was nominated as Best Album of the Year, and although it was not selected as the winner in the face of the strongest possible competition, Diana was nevertheless awarded the prize for the Best Jazz Vocal Performance, rocketing her to even greater fame. WHEN I LOOK IN YOUR EYES went on to become the best-selling jazz album in history until the release in September 2001 of THE LOOK OF LOVE, which became the first jazz album to debut on the Top Ten Billboard Chart. She was once again recognized at the Grammy Awards in February 2002 and at the Canadian Juno Awards in April with several more accolades.

Today, the young woman who once played to thin and mostly indifferent crowds at clubs in Nanaimo, Toronto, and Boston now plays to sellout crowds in theatres everywhere she goes: Paris, London, Tokyo, Sydney. In the process, she has built up a cadre of fans who adore her with an adulation equal to that accorded to high-profile pop and rock stars. Diana Krall has taken a position in the pantheon of Canadian women musicians beside Celine Dion, Shania Twain, Alanis Morissette, Sarah McLachlan, and Loreena McKennitt. This jazz diva has also become the center of a storm of controversy about whether her celebrity is the result of her own musical talent and dedication or the result of commercial image-making and packaging. And jazz critics are divided over the question of whether she is a true jazz artist or just a pop star.

———

That's the public record of the ordinary life yet remarkable achievement of Diana Krall, but I'm looking for more. I'd like to contact her family. I'd like to talk to her former high-school band teacher, Bryan Stovell. I search the telephone books, I try Directory Assistance, I look up their names on the internet. I try the Coastal Jazz and Blues Society, the organization which today administers the du Maurier Vancouver International Jazz Festival, because they have supported her career since the earliest days and she has often been featured on their stage. The small staff of this under-funded society is overwhelmed with work; my requests for information and photographs of Diana from her early years fall temporarily into the limbo of low priority, complicated by a computer failure which prevents my e-mails from reaching their proper destination.

A call to S.L. Feldman & Associates, the Vancouver company

that manages not only Diana Krall but also Joni Mitchell, puts me for several days on hold as I wait for Diana's road manager to come back to town. When he calls back, he says, "I'm going to pass this further up the food chain, to Steve or Sam." Steve is Steve Macklam, who became Diana's personal manager in 1994, and Sam is Sam Feldman himself, the owner of the company that bears his name. I'm glad to know that my project is important enough to merit their attention, but I hope I don't qualify as the diet on this particular food chain. A few days later, my fears are assuaged, even if my aims are not advanced much. A brief and genial conversation with Steve Macklam results in an agreement to send my resume along with a brief synopsis of my intentions in the book so that the company can decide how far they want to cooperate in this unofficial biography.

Several days later, I receive a call from Sam Feldman himself, since Steve Macklam is now out of town working on plans for Diana's tour of Europe and the United States. He is extremely courteous, but also slightly guarded. His approach makes his motives clear from the outset: he wants to protect the image of his singer, her privacy, her personal and artistic dignity. He expresses concern that Diana herself may not be in favor of a biography at this early stage in her career. The company might be interested later in an official biography, but that would depend upon many circumstances, including what he calls a "revenue stream." Most emphatically, he lets me know that everything would depend upon Diana's wishes. Mr. Feldman tells me that he has been burned previously by other biographers who made promises about what they would include in their books, but didn't keep them. He cites the example of a biographer of Joni Mitchell who said things hurtful to people close to Joni. He wants to protect Diana and her family. He nevertheless politely volunteers that I have every right to proceed. I let him know that my publisher has volunteered to send him a copy of the final manuscript before the book is published.

A few weeks later, S.L. Feldman & Associates sent me a package stuffed full of beautifully crafted publicity brochures, studio photographs, and, most importantly, a huge raft of photocopied articles and interviews from the international press — American, British, and Australian magazines — with photocopies of photographs I haven't seen before. While I had already surfed the internet for this kind of information, combed the clipping files at the Vancouver Public Library, and received from the Vancouver Island Regional Library in Nanaimo photocopies of all the articles they have on file about Diana, this package from her management company contained new and rare information, candid and revealing comments by Diana herself which opened new perspectives on her life and career.

The end result of following this lead to Diana Krall's management company was an answer that was neither yes nor no, neither totally friendly nor in any way hostile. Her management will not directly cooperate with my aims for now, but they won't stand in my way, either. I am grateful for Sam Feldman's candor and generosity. I have been treated courteously, arriving at a reasonable understanding with the company through his diplomatic intercession. I am also assured to know that Diana Krall is managed by capable people, who are genuinely concerned about her well-being. She is not in the least their instrument, manipulated at their will, which begins to color my take on the debate over her 'commercial' or 'pop' image. I doubt that this management company would — or perhaps even could — exploit her or her good will with her fans.

Now was the time to try my few personal contacts in Nanaimo. I called Ron Smith of Oolichan Books, a publisher of poetry and other titles out of Lantzville, a few miles north of Nanaimo. Oolichan had published my book, *Prez: Homage to Lester Young*, a suite of nine poems, some years before. Ron works at Malaspina University-College and probably has contact with people in the Music Department there, I reasoned, who probably had contact with Diana or with others who may help me to make connections.

"Sure," says Ron, "I know a couple of people. Give me a couple of days. I'll see what I can do."

Two days later, he calls me back. It turns out that a member of his staff, Linda Martin, actually knows Diana personally, and is a close friend of the Krall family. She likes my small book about Lester Young, and she's willing to take a copy of the book along with some interview questions to a party at the Krall residence and put them into Diana's hands. Our reasoning is that Diana might be more willing to cooperate if she reads and likes my book. I make sure in advance that Linda won't be jeopardizing her friendship or disturbing loyalties with the family by undertaking this mission on my behalf. Linda assures me the family "isn't like that at all" and they won't mind. "I'll just give her the book," she says, "and tell her what it's about and let her know the interview questions are inside, and leave it at that."

A few days later, I speak to Linda on the telephone. She tells me she handed over the package as planned. Diana responded, "Well, lots of people want to write my biography." Diana's mother added, playfully, "But *I* want to write your biography!" That's all that's said. Linda tells me that Diana leaves the party reading my book.

Ron Smith provides me with the names of some teachers in the Malaspina University-College Music Department who might have known Diana in the 1980s. I look up their e-mail addresses on the college website and send out some short requests. One professor writes back to say that he hardly knows Diana at all, but Steve Jones says he probably has some stories to relate. He is more than ready to talk, and he has his own reasons for wanting to do so. As one of the most enthusiastic music educators on the local Nanaimo scene, Steve is keen to advance the cause of music and help his students. Diana Krall is probably the biggest thing that has happened to music in Nanaimo in his lifetime, if not the entire history of the town. He tells me again what I already know: the person to reach is Bryan Stovell. He volunteers Bryan's precious telephone number without being asked.

A chance to meet with Bryan Stovell is ample reason in itself to make the trip from Vancouver to Nanaimo.

It's 7:00 a.m. on a British Columbia winter morning on the coast. The previous night there was one of the rare winter snowfalls that occur once or twice a year in the Vancouver region. By early morning the snow at lower altitudes has turned to rain, which has washed the last of the snow from the roads. The rain continues in the early morning dark and throughout the first hour of arriving dawn. I am traveling with my wife by car on the Upper Levels Highway, the portion of the Trans-Canada Highway connecting Vancouver with Horseshoe Bay, the terminal for the ferry which sets sail for Nanaimo on Vancouver Island at different hours throughout the day.

The ferry trip across the Strait of Georgia on the government-run B.C. Ferries takes more than an hour and half from the mainland departure point at Horseshoe Bay to the landing in Departure Bay in Nanaimo harbor. The B.C. ferries, carrying up to 2000 passengers and 400 cars each, sail out of Horseshoe Bay toward Nanaimo every two hours during daylight and just as often in the opposite direction. Every two hours, the main streets of the town of Nanaimo are choked with cars, trucks, and motorcycles headed through the city for points south, west, and north on Vancouver Island.

The panoramic view of the Georgia Strait from the higher levels of the sweeping roadway of the Upper Levels Highway is always spectacular in any weather. The full circular vista takes in a huge arena of ocean and mountain geography, including Vancouver's Point Grey and the further reaches of Tswassen, the Gulf Islands between the mainland and Vancouver, the peaks of the Washington Olympic Peninsula, and the highest peaks of the Vancouver Island mountain ranges. On clear days, the snow on the tops of these mountains is actually visible, miles distant. Today, in the rain, they are covered in gray cloud.

Half way between our home and the ferry terminal, we are hit by a sudden squall of pelting rain mixed with snowy slush, just at the moment in the day when dark and the rising light make the visible world least securely visible. The drivers of the cars swishing by in the blinding rain are making no concession to the reduced visibility or the slippery highway awash with streams of slushy rainwater. They barrel through triumphantly at full legal speed and more, their taillights blurring in the wake of spray thrown up by their tires. This is the normal rush to catch the ferry. These drivers have no wish to be left behind to wait for two hours in the rainy parking lot for a second ferry if they should miss the first one. A few minutes of this cloudburst and we pass mercifully out from under the black clouds into a lighter gray sky. The rain lets up, though not completely, turns to a fine drizzle. Already the clouds are beginning to fragment and break up: the sun may yet shine today.

Within minutes, we have paid our fare and are in the line-up to board the ferry. The cars from Nanaimo are already driving out of the ferry's big dark belly and off the ramp on their way to Vancouver and points east. Soon enough, we are boarding the ferry ourselves, on our way to Nanaimo and Vancouver Island where we hope to begin filling in details of this portrait of Diana Krall .

The weather is already changing as we board the ferry, as it often does on the West Coast, from sun to rain, to sun, to rain and back again throughout the day, clouds breaking up and circulating through the sky. The clouds are already lightening in the dawn, patches of blue are beginning to appear amidst the gray. The tops of mountains become visible out of the low-lying clouds. A halo of sunlight outlines their ridges, glowing bright golden. The sun has not yet risen over the tops of the mountains, though. In the next few minutes, we witness one of the most spectacular, but at the same time, most common events in the British Columbia landscape and weather. The clouds obscuring the mountains begin to thin out and evaporate, patches breaking off from the body of a cloud, becoming thin, mobile wisps before vanishing entirely in the chilly air. The water of the channel, formerly a uniform gun-metal gray furled with endless waves, turns to a sparkling azure, marked by countless bright whitecaps.

The ferry patrons, according to long-established custom, wait patiently in long lines at the cafeteria for breakfast. The ferry is lightly patronized today — less than half the seats are full — yet the line on both sides of the cafeteria counter is 20 yards long. Within half an hour, all of these people have been served. They sit back to enjoy their breakfast and the view.

Georgia Strait, from its center, appears as a huge, slightly convex circle of indigo, miles wide and thousands of feet deep, surrounded by gray and azure mountains and clouds. The mountains in the distance seem to reach back into the deepest space, range after range: water, mountain, cloud, mountain, cloud, clear sky, the tips of the mountains lined with bright bands of light, gray shadows underneath cut through with other swaths of light, shadow and light in a slow but constant interplay.

Ferry travel in British Columbia is unlike any other form of travel. In good weather, passengers are free to stroll the decks and feel the sunshine and the wind in their hair and on their faces. The speed of travel is slow, so there is time to dwell on detail: the way the skyline of the city grows smaller in perspective, the gradual appearance of distant landmarks. The ferry trip provides 90 minutes of respite. The faces and the posture of passengers visibly relax during the passage. Soon after setting out, people begin to read books and newspapers, play cards, work quietly on lap-top computers, talk softly on cell phones, tend to their children, wander the aisles or the decks, seek out familiar faces, cover their faces and doze. Separated from mainland cares, passengers are free to observe others as they themselves are observed, mildly, with simple human curiosity.

On board the ferry, there are government workers in pinstripe dress shirts. Commuting for reasons connected with their work, they study documents from their briefcases, concentrate over their lap-top computers. Others are dressed in their normal day clothes — jackets with union affiliations or company names emblazoned on them, buttons advertising their opposition to the recent government measures, baseball caps, blue-jeans. A Punjabi family, the men wearing turbans, the women dressed in elegant white saris, their heads covered with white shawls, sits together comfortably in a complex of corner seats. Two native couples are eating together in the cafeteria, talking and smiling. Standing on the deck are men with thick moustaches, bushy beards, loggers, fishermen, and hippies, strong West-Coast and Vancouver-Island individuals, where individualism is tolerated, even welcome. The typical British Columbia crowd on a typical British Columbia ferry.

Ferry rides are part of being at home in British Columbia, something that West Coast people love to do, something that enriches life, something that Diana Krall and her parents have undoubtedly done many times together, enjoying the ride among their fellow British Columbians.

———

In September 1996, Diana Krall's third album, ALL FOR YOU, was featured in *Time* magazine, a cause for celebration in her hometown but also a cause of consternation when Nanaimo was referred to as "suburb of Vancouver." Elsewhere, Diana's hometown has been called "backwoods Nanaimo."

Nanaimo, a town of 70,000 people on Vancouver Island, is neither a suburb of Vancouver, nor is it in the backwoods of British Columbia. At least 25 miles of sea water separate the city of Nanaimo from Vancouver in the British Columbia mainland. After Victoria, the capital city of British Columbia, Nanaimo is the second largest and the second oldest city on Vancouver Island, where the weather is sunny throughout the year, almost Mediteranean, never too hot, never too cold.

Vancouver Island is the largest island on the west coast of the Pacific. The separation between Vancouver Island and the mainland lies directly over the fault line of the same two tectonic plates that create the famed San Andreas fault running the length of the North American and South American Cordillera. The shape of the east coast of the Island, like a piece from a giant jigsaw puzzle, betrays the fact that it was once part of the mainland, separated now for centuries by geological activity vast in time and space. The Gulf Islands, a scattering of smaller islands between the mainland and the larger island, are further pieces in the jigsaw puzzle, further evidence of this ancient separation.

The 285 mile length and the 12,408 square miles of the Island embrace wide geographical and climatic differences, even though the weather on the Island is mostly temperate summer and winter, and snow is rare along the coastlines, even on the northern coast in winter. The climatologists tell us that this temperate clime is owing to the warmth carried in the Gulf Stream, arms of which circulate around both the eastern and western sides of the Island.

The climate of the settled part of the island is warm in summer, cooler, but still temperate, in winter. The fall and winter weather is also often wet and rainy and foggy. Storms roll in from the Pacific every five days or so, and the moving air, driven upwards by the obstacle of the mountains running down the center of the island, cools in the upper atmosphere. Water vapor contained in the air from evaporation on the vast Pacific condenses over the mountains, forming clouds that drop their burden of moisture on the east coast of the island in nearly regular cycles of mostly mild rain and sunshine.

These rainstorms provide the immense tons of water necessary for sustaining the growth of the rainforests of the island. The island is a mighty earth garden of big firs and cedars, pines, spruce, yew, and arbutus. The trees of this rain forest, especially the big forests of Douglas fir, when converted into lumber, are the mainstay of the Island economy, the basis of the island's connection to the wider world, historically and for the foreseeable future. Today, most of the forest on Vancouver Island is second growth — that is to say, the island has been logged almost end to end once already. In the early days, the lumber from the island forests provided the raw material for the wooden ships of the ship-building industry in Britain in the nineteenth century, as well as the lumber to build the new pioneer communities up and down the British Columbia coast, frontier outposts of the nineteenth-century British empire. The new forest growth, which has sprung up in the intervening years, is now being logged a second time, providing lumber for the domestic housing industry, but also for shipping in unprocessed form to the United States, Japan, and the rest of the world. The few remaining stands of previously unlogged old growth forest have become a battleground between the mostly American owned logging companies active in the province today and the growing force of the British Columbia environmentalists struggling to save the forest for aesthetic and spiritual reasons. The struggles of the B.C. environmentalists to save the old growth forests at Clayoquot Sound on the Vancouver Island's west coast have made Vancouver Island, especially the Island's wilder western coast, a focus of the international environmental movement.

For all their pragmatic economic connection to the natural resources of the island, Vancouver Islanders, like British Columbians in general, also nourish in their souls an aesthetic and spiritual connection to the natural environment. British Columbians are "nature freaks," even if they live in cities. Even the most avid supporter of the logging industry will speak longingly and rhapsodically about the beauty of the forest and the sea, of the need for a human connection to the land and nature. Islanders and British Columbians in general were once mostly loggers and fishers, even if today they are highly urbanized city-dwellers. In recreation mode, these urbanized British Columbia citizens are still campers, hikers, country joggers, downhill skiers, cross-country skiers, snowboarders, boaters, sailors, recreational fishers, kayakers, mountaineers, spelunkers, wind surfers, surf surfers, horseback riders. Diana Krall, herself a horseback rider, a swimmer, and a skier, is no exception — an Islander and British Columbian to the bone.

The human population of the Vancouver Island is close to 600,000, but most of this population is concentrated in a thin coastal line running from Victoria at the south-western tip of the Island, up the Island Highway along the very edge of the eastern coast from south to north. The farther north one drives, the more sparse the population becomes, the smaller the towns, and the greater the distance between them, the thinner the veneer of civilization and settlement, the more rural and unsettled, finally ending in outright wilderness along the north-eastern coast. Although the south-east coast of the Island has been settled for more than 150 years, the remoter parts of the Island even today exist in the midst of a vast wilderness unoccupied by human beings, even though they may be no more than 50 or 60 miles away from a larger urban center with all the amenities of modern life.

The populated east coast of the island is separated from the sparsely settled west coast by a series of tall, snow-capped mountain ranges. Although the island is criss-crossed by logging roads, there are hardly any roads connecting the east coast with the west coast, and most of them are dusty, dirt roads or logging roads that run like the webs of spiders through the rain-forests in the central island. Some of the remote communities on the west coast of the island can only be reached by these dirt logging roads — some cannot be reached by road at all. Highways to tourist destinations like Long Beach and Tofino on the west coast have only been built in the last 40 years. Between the west coast of the Island and Japan, there are only thousands of miles of sea water, filled with big waves rolling onto the coast. Surfers come from around the world to test these waves in their wet suits. The water here is bone-chillingly cold, unlike the water on the eastern coast of the Island, which is warm, almost tropical. On the southern ends of the Gulf Islands in the heat of summer, there is a fragrance as though of flowers borne in the wind from somewhere deep in the Pacific. The north coast in winter is lashed by huge gales off the Pacific, and the entries to the inlets of the coast — Barkley Sound, Clayoquot Sound, Nootka Sound, Kyoquot Sound, Quatsino Sound — are known as the graveyards of many boats and ships large and small.

The mountains and the rain forest are filled with wild life of every kind — deer, cougar, bear, marmots, raccoons, squirrels,

Stellar jays, Canada Geese, whistler swans, grebes, loons, ducks of all kinds, swallows, sparrows, juncos, flocks of sandpipers, and huge numbers of hummingbirds, especially on the west coast. The waters of the Strait of Georgia were once filled with innumerable salmon and are still home for numerous seals, sea lions, dolphins, and several diminishing pods of resident killer whales. From anywhere on Vancouver Island, even from the most settled cities like Nanaimo and Victoria, the power of this wilderness is always present only a few minutes away. Experience of the power and beauty of this wilderness has been part of the life and consciousness of every Vancouver Island inhabitant since the island was first settled 150 years ago.

Nanaimo was one of the first regions to be settled. The area was explored by the Spanish, who are commemorated in the names of the Gulf Islands in the Strait of Georgia: Saturna, Valdes, Gabriola, Galiano. Captain Cook was the first Englishman to explore the region, followed in the eighteenth century by Captain Vancouver, whose name was given to the island and the province's largest city on the mainland. Coal was discovered in the region in the 1850s, a business associated with the name of the Scottish miner Robert Dunsmuir, who not only owned several mines, but was instrumental in building of the Island continuation of the transcontinental Canadian Pacific Railway, operating the Esquimalt and Nanaimo Railway, which still runs daily between Nanaimo and the Victoria suburb of Esquimalt. Today the earth under the city of Nanaimo is still honeycombed by miles of abandoned mine shafts.

Diana Krall's parents came from working class families of long-time residents of Nanaimo. Steve Krall, Diana's paternal grandfather, ran a small but popular restaurant called Steve's Coffee Bar in downtown Nanaimo, which can be seen on an Arts and Minds video from Bravo. Diana triumphantly claims, alluding to the life story of another singer, Loretta Lynn: "I'm a coalminer's granddaughter and proud of it." Even if Diana's parents had desired to follow the footsteps of her grandfather into the depths of the coal mine, historical circumstances would have prevented the possibility: the coal industry in North America collapsed in the 1950s with the advent of the ready availability of petroleum fuels, diesel engines for trains, and gas and oil heating. The coalmines in Nanaimo, formerly the main source of the city's employment, slowly petered out and were finally shut down. The last commercial coal was taken from Nanaimo in the early 1950s, and the town might have become a ghost town, like many other mining towns in British Columbia, if it had not become a center for the transportation for the lumber and pulp industries.

Nanaimo has a reputation as a tough, working-class town. There are still muscled men in mackinaws and caulk boots in the downtown bars, loud loggers and quieter fishers, drinking beer, playing pool, but more and more residents are professionals and business people. Entering Nanaimo from the ferry or passing through from south to north, the town appears like any other town of comparable size in North America, with used-car dealerships, fast-food restaurants, and flat-roofed warehouses stretched out alongside the highway, all built in the last 30 years.

Since its first days of settlement, Nanaimo has been a multicultural community. First there were the natives of the Coast Salish nation who called the place *Sneneymexw* (roughly pronounced Sneynomo, from which the present name is derived), meaning the 'meeting place'. After the Spanish explorers, the English and the Scottish were the first to come to the region as settlers, followed by the Chinese, who were imported to work as indentured laborers on the railroad and in Dunsmuir's mines. The records displayed in the mining museum in nearby Cumberland list the names of hundreds of Chinese miners killed in accidents and cave-ins, alongside the names of tens of Scottish, English, Polish, and Italian miners. Later came East Indians, mostly Punjabis, who have worked in the sawmills and pulp mills in the region. Subsequent waves of immigration following the two world wars of our century have swelled the population and enhanced the ethnic mix. Now nicknamed 'The Hub City', Nanaimo is not only a place at the center of a transportation wheel, with spokes connecting the Island to the mainland and neighboring towns, but

also a multicultural center, with many ethnic groups living har-
moniously together. Surprisingly, this town is also a center for
young jazz artists.

The friends we are visiting in Nanaimo live on an island suburb of
the city, inaccessible by bridge. The only way to reach them on
Protection Island is via a jaunty little ferry, which leaves hourly from
the inner harbor of Nanaimo and takes ten minutes to reach the
smaller island. Our hosts have told us they would meet us at 12:10
p.m. on Sunday. We have arrived three hours early, which gives us
lots of time to explore the city. Because it is Sunday morning, the
smaller stores in town are closed. We have promised to take some
cheese to our friends for our lunch together, so we have to find a
store to buy it. Only the major mall in town is open, with a newly-
opened casino nearby. We make our way to the mall on foot. In the
mall, outside a restaurant, we find a newspaper box, and in the newspaper box is a copy of the local newspaper, *The Nanaimo Daily News*,
whose headline announces that two Nanaimo citizens have earned
cultural honors. In the upper right-hand corner of the front page appears a thumbnail photograph of a man cradling a saxophone in his
arms. It is none other than Malaspina University-College music instructor, Steve Jones. Only three days previously, I had spoken to
him on the telephone from Vancouver. I knew from our conversation that he was an active force on the local music scene, that he had
once had contact with Diana Krall when she was a teenager, and had
worked with her and a band from the college he once instructed.
But I had never expected to see his face on the front page of the
Nanaimo newspaper minutes after my arrival. Perhaps the tourist
brochure published on the internet advertising the town is telling
the truth when it says, "Musically, Nanaimo has been dubbed 'jazz
city', and not only because it is home to divas Diana Krall and Ingrid
Jensen! Local musicians perform at coffee houses, restaurants,
nightclubs and pubs across the city almost every night, providing
diners with a plethora of musical styles to state [sic] the senses."

A charming story Jones had told me over the telephone was of a young Diana, barely 14 years old. In those days, Jones was a new instructor at the College. With a new band he put together, he sallied out to play a daytime concert at the Woodlands Junior Secondary School in Nanaimo. They played a set of jazz and other standards. The band was afterwards approached by a personable 14-year-old, who quietly asked if she might sit in with them for while on the electric piano. The boys in the band were sceptical, Steve recalled, and told the youngster they were working on some pretty hard and complicated musical charts, but they finally relented. Within minutes, they were standing around the electric piano with their mouths open, astonished at the skill in Diana's quick fingers, with her ability to read the charts, to keep time, and to provide a swinging piano accompaniment to the band. Thereafter, they were glad to have her play with them whenever she wanted.

Later, around 1980 or 1981, Diana joined the Malaspina College Big Band, and Steve Jones worked with her there. Under the influence of her early mentor, high-school band teacher Bryan Stovell, she also played with the Nanaimo Musicians' Association big band. Once directed by Stovell, the Musicians' Association Band is now under Jones' direction, and it was partly on this account that he was written up in the Saturday edition of the *Nanaimo Daily News*.

Strangely, despite her overarching prominence on the local musical scene, Diana's name doesn't occur in the article at all. Nor do the names of other Nanaimo students Steve Jones has taught: the trumpeter Ingrid Jensen and her sister Christine; Phil Dwyer, a prominent Canadian saxophonist; Pamela York, a jazz pianist who now works in San Diego; Karen Graves of the Mother of Pearl, a jazz-oriented band working in Vancouver.

But the first clues of where Diana comes from musically are already beginning to appear within my first few moments in the town. Before our trip to Nanaimo, I spoke by telephone to Gary Gaudet, a freelance writer working out of Nanaimo. Steve Jones informed me that Gaudet had written an article connected with

Diana, collecting some old photographs while also talking to a lot of local people who knew Diana in the early days. As it turned out, Gaudet's interest was not only directed toward Diana Krall, but also toward the development of music culture in Nanaimo generally. He was currently in the process of marketing his article to *Down Beat*. In Gaudet's view, the appearance of Diana Krall, however welcome, was perhaps only the most dramatic instance of an on-going music scene. According to Gaudet, the music of Nanaimo reaches right back to the arrival of the miners from Britain in the nineteenth century, and forward to music educators like Steve Jones and Bryan Stovell, connected to Central Island High School and to the music program at Malaspina University-College, where Steve Jones works as a full-time instructor and Bryan Stovell as a part-time instructor in his retirement.

Steve Jones is the model of a Nanaimo musical educator. Like many other musicians of his generation, he decided to become a musician in 1964, the same year Diana was born, when he saw the Beatles on the *Ed Sullivan Show*. "Everybody was picking up instruments and starting up garage bands after that," he says. "Your parents would always tell you to 'take something to fall back on'," and for me that was education. But the first day of my practicum I just felt, 'I'm home, I've arrived' and I've felt that way about teaching ever since. It was a defining moment. I realized that I'd maybe never play in the big time, never go to New York City to make my name as a musician. I liked teaching so much I had to go that way. I just couldn't imagine doing anything else." He says he enjoys the chances to work with students who may well someday become household names like Diana. "You know who they are almost immediately, when you hear them perform," he says, "and you have to let them know, help them live up to their potential."

Jones is a member of the ten-piece jazz funk band called Decadence and a member of the Nanaimo Music Association big band which holds regular shows in town, summer music workshops at the Malaspina Summer Jazz Academy and in towns from Smithers, a remote northern British Columbia town, to Whitehorse, Yukon. He also plays college jam events at the Queen's Hotel in central Nanaimo, at the Harewood Arms Inn, and at the Acme Food Co. restaurant downtown. Jones had been selected by the organizers of the New Offshore Jazz Series for the honor of leading the band that, on the Friday before our arrival in Nanaimo, opened up the new series of performances at the Coast Bastion Inn, where Diana also played solo piano during the 1980s. Joel Prévost, who has been bringing internationally famous jazz artists to Nanaimo for years, pays tribute to the musical abilities of Jones and other musical educators. "We often don't recognize the level of talent of those who have chosen to be in the academic world," Provost says. "We wanted to give him the recognition he deserves here because he is definitely of the calibre to be in a line-up like this."

On the front cover of the most recent issue of *Jazz Times*, which bills itself as "America's Jazz Magazine," there appears a photograph of Diana Krall, announcing her as the winner of the *Jazz Times* Reader Poll as the year's best jazz singer. In the same issue, there also appears a short review of BLUE YORK, the recent CD release by pianist Pamela York, another graduate from the Malaspina University-College jazz program. The author notes that York comes from Nanaimo, "the same unlikely burg that produced Diana Krall and the trumpeter Ingrid Jensen." He wonders parenthetically: "Is there something in the water there?" Within half an hour of our arrival in Nanaimo, we are already beginning to discover what it is that the water around Nanaimo contains — a mighty dose of musical knowledge and feeling infused by generations of dedicated musicians and musical educators living in the town.

Evelyn Hepinstall, a long-time jazz fan and Nanaimo resident, who used to hear Diana play at different restaurants in town, explains just how deep music education runs in this region. She recently attended a fundraising "Jazz Fest" featuring two well-known professional jazz musicians from the region, Ross Taggart and Hugh Fraser. The main participants were high-school and junior high-school bands, Grade VIII and Grade IX music students. "To hear those kids at that very young age playing so well," says Evelyn, "well, it was just amazing." Bryan Stovell, Diana's high-school band teacher, later remarks to me on the telephone that Nanaimo District Secondary and Malaspina University-College graduates like Diana Krall and Ingrid Jensen have brought more positive attention to the town in recent years than the annual bathtub races that used to be the main event for tourists traveling to Nanaimo.

Gary Gaudet's observations on the Nanaimo music scene were confirmed by many things I saw and by everyone I spoke to in Nanaimo. Two days later, I visited the Port Theatre where Diana has held triumphant homecoming concerts. "The flowers, the flowers, that's what I remember," says Sandra Thomson, recalling Diana Krall's last concert in the Port Theatre. Thomson is Acting Manager of the Port Theatre, and she is showing me around the Margaret Strongitherm Gallery on the floor of theatre, talking about the history of music in Nanaimo and Diana Krall's place within the music culture here.

The Port Theatre in downtown Nanaimo is part of a cultural and commercial complex of new buildings, which the City Council of the Nanaimo commissioned to be built in 1998 in the hope of revitalizing the downtown core. The theatre is the most modern building in the entire downtown area. The big white cube of the body of the theatre is 50 feet high, conjoined at the front of the building by a round element, the lobby complex, whose most visible feature is a web of buttresses in wood and aluminum. The iconic representation of the building on the theatre's logo suggests the bridge of a ship, or a lighthouse on shore. The building is situated on a red brick terrace. On the same terrace is found the Nanaimo and District Public Library. Not far away on a bluff is the Nanaimo Civic Museum.

Sandra Thomson describes the two sold-out benefit concerts Diana played on October 5 and October 6 last year to help raise money to buy a new Steinway & Sons grand piano for the theatre. The concert sold out both nights at $175 a ticket, and raised $25,000, about half the purchase cost of the new piano. The grateful citizens of Nanaimo brought flowers to shower on Diana, the much beloved daughter of their city. "There were so many flowers, so many bouquets," Thomson says, "that when Diana and her family went to the elevator to leave the theatre after the post-concert reception, there was no room for human beings in the elevator. There were too many flowers, pots and pots of them!"

Sandra shows me around the gallery where Diana's picture is displayed alongside the photographs of other Nanaimo citizens who have made important contributions to the cultural and musical life of the city. There is a photograph of Ingrid Jensen, the jazz trumpet phenomenon and graduate from Malaspina University-College music program, dressed in black leather and holding her trumpet. Bryan Stovell is there in an individual photograph directly beside the photograph of the 41 members of the Nanaimo Concert Band, 41 men and women posed gracefully on a green meadow, surrounded by lush Vancouver Island forest, holding their trumpets, trombones, and woodwinds, in celebration of an award given to the band on the occasion of the 125th anniversary of its founding. The caption next to the photograph announces that the band, first founded in 1872, is the oldest continuously active band of its kind in all of Canada. Stovell is remembered in this gallery, not only for his contributions to the concert band, but as "one of the most gifted musical educators in B.C." Isabel and Alastair Highet, a couple credited with introducing the Kodaly System of Music to Nanaimo in 1980, are also recognized. The Kodaly system they established was so successful that within a few years the use of the system had spread to all of Canada. This same couple in 1965 established a music program known as "Sound of Singing," which grew to include 12,000 students across the country. Among others honored is Joyce Horner, Diana's former piano teacher, a dignified woman in glasses seated near a piano. She was inducted into this gallery of musicians and artists in 1997, a year before her student was so recognized.

Sandra Thomson tells me that the gallery isn't finished yet — the funds still haven't come through to pay the cost of completing the building. The B.C. government has recently announced deep cost-cutting measures. Because of the increasing shift to job-related education, Thomson fears the arts programs in the schools and the cultural institutions like the Port Theatre will be severely curtailed. "The teachers and the specialists will no longer be there," Thomson says, to nurture young artists like Diana Krall. There will be no more flowers. The theatre will no longer hear even the ghosts of the miners who came off the boats a century ago holding their horns in their hands.

———

My friends on Protection Island have provided me with a few more names of people who have known Diana. Ross Fraser works out of an office on the local college campus as a cultural director. As part of his job, Fraser is in charge of raising funds for cultural events. He met Diana in 1995 when he organized a fundraiser for a college music program in which Diana appeared as featured performer just before she was first nominated for a Grammy award. Mr. Fraser recalls the sumptuous crystal and linen banquet he had a hand in organizing for prominent Nanaimo citizens and business people. The guests were served a gourmet meal prepared by the internationally recognized culinary school at the college. The participants paid $75 a head for tickets in those days for the meal and entertainment. After the meal, the donors made their way a few yards across the campus to the college theatre, where Diana performed. Most had never heard of her before, most of them didn't know her name, and some of the donors didn't like the music very much. One businessman remarked afterwards that he'd rather have heard a concert delivered by someone like Gary Fjellgaard, a well-known folksinger from the region. Two years later, the same people were ready to pony up

$175 for the benefit at the Port Theatre, where Diana performed, this time to raise money to buy a grand piano for the theatre. No one complained about the entertainment that night.

Scott Littlejohn, the owner of B[astion] C[ity] Recording Ltd., recalls his early encounters with Diana when he made her first recordings as she prepared demonstration tapes for potential employers. My own meeting with Littlejohn was a sample of the kind of response Nanaimo citizens are ready to provide whenever Diana's name is mentioned. By chance alone, I had stepped into the small studio facility of the CIVI television station, where I spoke to the station manager, Bruce Williams, asking him for information about Diana. Littlejohn was working in a glass booth as the audio operator for Williams' *New Day* breakfast program. As soon as he heard the name of Diana Krall, he came bounding out of his booth to offer his assistance. Littlejohn has an intimate connection with the Nanaimo musical community through his activities as a studio instructor at Malaspina University-College; he's also been a friend of Diana and her family for many years. He agreed to provide me with as much information as I could ask for, once he had consulted with Diana's parents for their permission. He called Adella Krall to ask her permission, and she said, "Go ahead, talk your head off, say anything you want."

"I operate a recording studio here in Nanaimo," Scott begins his account, "and have since 1980. During the 20 plus years of recording Island artists, I recall with fondness working on the first early sessions with a then teenaged Diana Krall. Diana was in high school then and I received a call to record some piano demos for her. I had heard rumors of a great young jazz pianist coming up through the school band program. I was unprepared for the level of ability I was about to hear.

"My studio in those days was located in the back half of a music store, a few miles from Diana's home overlooking Departure Bay. The day of the first session I met a very polite and friendly girl, but one who was very nervous, not overly confident. After small talk and an effort to get Diana to feel relaxed, she strolled over to the piano to warm up. It was then that I heard the makings of the piano player she has become. She played like someone much older, and with the passion most players would envy. As long as she was playing, she was in another place, focused completely on her music. As soon as she stopped, she suddenly became aware of the rest of us (two or three people — likely her Mom or Dad or Bryan Stovell — I wish I could recall), and immediately became self-conscious, as though it wouldn't be up to the standard we were used to hearing."

As Littlejohn continues, "the recording we did that day was a few instrumentals, dumped onto cassette for her critiquing. I went home full of stories to my wife about the amazing young pianist I'd heard that day. A short time later another session was set up, this time a bit more ambitious in its goal. This time the demo was to send around to restaurants to get some payin' playin'. I think this session was produced by Rick Kilburn, a well-known jazz bassist who'd just come back to the Island after a few successful years doing high-end session work in New York. At some point during what was supposed to be another instrumental session, Diana started singing along with a song she was rehearsing. The effect on us in the control room was immediate — Wow!! Even as a teenager, Diana sang like a sultry mature woman. We kept hearing a sound that didn't match the picture of the person singing it. It was most disarming. She was very self-conscious and self critical about her singing, though by this time she was able to admit that maybe she could allow herself a bit of pride about her playing abilities — but never in a boastful way.

"Diana finished school, then took off to take private lessons with various well-known teachers and mentors. Over the next few years, I would see her when she came to town, mixing sound for her if she had a local gig that needed sound reinforcement. By this time she had discovered her voice, and was getting comfy with her style. Looking back on it, it seems awfully funny because she was always so grateful that I would consent to do sound for her! I say that because she was always so humble, even as she was starting to become regionally 'known'. The last time I mixed for her was for a special 25th anniversary concert for Malaspina University-College's Alumni. By this time, she had an album and a record deal, but hadn't crossed over to the mass audience outside of the jazz world. She flew in from New York with a trio, and played a smokin' set that thrilled the 'jazz' folks but left some of the 'CCR' [Creedence Clearwater Revival] crowd a bit mystified.

"Several years went by and I only saw her from the paying audience, like everyone else, when she came to town. I'd hear bits and pieces of her successes and goings on from Jim or Adella when I'd see them around town. During the fall of 2000, her sister Michelle got married. Adella called and asked if I could set up the sound gear for Diana to perform a song with during the reception, to be held at a small waterfront lodge south of Nanaimo. I was given her Vancouver representative's number, who sent over a list of equipment requirements. I remember thinking that Diana had sure come a long way to have handlers sending over detailed overkill equipment needs for an intimate, one song performance. I arranged the necessary gear and went out to the picturesque location to set up. I hadn't spoken to Diana for a few years and was looking forward to seeing how she was doing. Admittedly, I was a little nervous that with her new fame that something wouldn't be to her liking with the equipment and it would but a cramp in her style.

"I just got everything working when she walked into the reception room early in the morning of the wedding day. She gave me an enthusiastic hug, asked how my wife and kids were, then looked at the array of stand-mounted speakers and the large stage monitor by the piano and — gulp — frowned. She then said something to the effect of, 'I don't need all this s —, let's just keep it really simple and get most of this stuff out of here.' She then got a coffee from the lodge staff and sat down to play and sing a bit for the other early morning folks assembling the last minute wedding decorations for the room. She may be at the top of her game, and internationally famous, but she didn't seem any different than the amazing talent I'd been lucky enough to be associated with so many years before. On that day she'd just finished a tour, and had been hanging out in L.A. with her friend Sir Elton while he was recording his last album. In the few minutes I had to chat with her, she told me a few anecdotes about other music legends she's spent time with. She's now a confident, consummate performer, but still manages to balance her new life with a small-town attitude."

———————

A day later, I'm standing outside the Queen's Hotel on Victoria Crescent downtown, checking out the posters advertising the acts playing there. I've read somewhere that Diana might have played the Queen's at some time in the 1980s. I want to have a look. A signboard outside the Hotel tells me that the bar in the Queen's features jazz jams on Monday evenings. Today is Monday. I now know exactly what I'll be doing this evening.

To kill the two hours before the show begins, I take a walk through downtown Nanaimo. Because the downtown core is built on several levels, finding your way from one level to another is somewhat like navigating through a maze — access is given from some directions, but not from others. On the map, the streets are laid out in a kind of spider-web pattern, bending toward the harbor on the southern and northern ends, crossed diagonally by roads from the east and west. The roads bend at every corner, odd streets break off and go in odd directions. Having passed the front end of some landmark like the museum or the Ports Theatre, the wanderer unaccountably finds himself coming by surprise on the back end of the same building, not knowing how the maze of streets might have brought him there. On the southern edge of the downtown core, there is a pocket of old housing, gray but charming houses in slightly ramshackle condition, once perhaps the homes of miners or pulp workers. The buildings in the downtown core have a reassuring antique quality, but many of the shops are closed, their windows covered over with paper. I'm sticking to one of the main downtown commercial streets so as not go get too badly turned around. Suddenly, coming down the street in front of me is an oddly familiar-looking figure — a kind of apparition really, in his battered hat and long gray weather-stained trench coat. With his ruck-sack hanging on his shoulder and his gray hair and beard flowing around him as he walks, it's none other than Tim Lander, an itinerant street poet I've known for years. He looks a little like Coleridge's Ancient Mariner, though his eyes are more like those of a benign Santa Claus than the mad eyes of the Mariner.

Tim is an unrepentant survivor of the rebellious 1960s, a hippie elder, a bearded wiseman, a social outsider and a mild-mannered rebel. There are many of these survivors of the '60s spread throughout British Columbia, especially on Vancouver Island, partly because the locals extend a high level of tolerance to social difference, partly because the loggers and fishers who made up the base population of the coast have always been more than slightly wild, and also because the working class culture of the region has its deepest roots in the British working class of the nineteenth century. Tim is representative of that culture, with its working class politics and its broad humanitarianism. Working-class folksongs were popular in the urban centers of the province in early '60s, and even now, a local bar in some remote B.C. town will sometimes feature a guitarist-singer picking out these songs.

Tim has obviously never felt the need to change the style he adopted when he came from England in his youth fresh from unhappy experiences in the English army, experiences which only confirmed him in his earlier pacifist convictions. His most recent book of poems examines the effect on his family of the loss of his father, lost in action in Europe during World War II. He came to the west coast of Canada seeking freedom from the intensities of English society. His beard and dress work as a kind of protective coloring: they serve to keep off triflers. The conventionally-minded, the narrow-minded, in a word, the tight-assed, will turn away from Tim's appearance in distaste or even disgust. I've seen it happen more than once myself. But this is their own loss. Anyone open-minded enough to stop and talk with him soon discovers an intelligent, knowledgeable, well-read, and humane personality, one of the last of the Ragged-Trousered Philanthropists.

Together, Tim and I agree to go for a beer. He takes me to a small pub on a side street called The Cobble Stone, which turns out to be a typical Vancouver Island pub. Men and women dressed in biker leathers, a few tough-looking men in worker's clothes, bright jackets and baseball hats, a pool table at the back. It's early in the evening, so the place is mostly empty, though some of the people are already slightly drunk. Some of the patrons make friendly remarks to Tim, tipping their glasses in his direction, recognizing him as one of them. Tim tells me that last Saturday evening The Cobble Stone was the scene of a poetry reading by Governor General's Award winning poet Patrick Lane, visiting from Saanichton near Victoria, and other local poets, including Tim himself. That must have been a busy cultural night in Nanaimo, I thought, with Steve Jones' band playing at the Coast Bastion lounge. Tim tells me that Nanaimo is the bookstore center of Vancouver Island, maybe Canada. "More books and bookstores here in Nanaimo than in any other city of the same size in Canada," he says. Together over our beer, we exchange literary gossip and complaints about publishers and other matters of interest to literary folk like ourselves.

I tell him what I've discovered about the music culture of Nanaimo, about Gary Gaudet's still unpublished article about the nineteenth-century coal miners, the musical instruments they brought with them from overseas, the chorus they founded in Nanaimo. I tell him about my encounter with Steve Jones at the Malaspina music department earlier in the day. I tell him I'm going to attend the jam at the Queen's Hotel later in the evening, and he tells me, "Oh, yeah, the students from the college jazz program sometimes play there on Monday nights." In his ongoing role as a concerned Nanaimo citizen, Tim pronounces owlishly that the music program at Malaspina University-College is the "best thing at the college — along with the aquaculture program and the culinary program, of course." He praises Steve Jones for his efforts to build the program and bring it to the attention of the public. "The 'City Fathers' here in Nanaimo, as they call them, are more keen on real-estate than they are on music and culture," says Tim. "You'd think with all the attention that people like Diana Krall bring to the music and culture in the city, they'd get the point. But nothing ever changes, on that front. The artists are always left to scratch and starve." It's a theme I'll hear again from Bryan Stovell later in the week.

When we're done with our beer and our conversation, Tim insists on walking me to the Coast Bastion Inn where I intend to interview the bartender before heading back to the show at the Queen's. In my chance encounter with Scott Littlejohn, he had told me I would soon enough find that every Nanaimo citizen I met would stake a claim to having a memory of Diana while she lived in town. Among all the hundreds of newspaper and internet clippings I've read, there is one that mentions the Coast Bastion as the site of Saturday evening shows featuring Diana on piano. The Coast Bastion Hotel, at 14 stories tall, is one of the tallest buildings on the Nanaimo downtown landscape. Except for a highrise apartment building a few blocks away, the rest of Nanaimo is old buildings offices, stores, restaurants, mostly two stories tall, rarely three and never four. The Coast Bastion is one of the most modern buildings in town. There are plenty of windows, plenty of air and space, consistent with the effort to create a touristy atmosphere of sun and sea. The lobby is almost completely empty and the west coast seafood restaurant is absolutely deserted. The bar has only one lonely patron, who soon enough finishes his drink and is gone.

The woman bartender is standing quietly behind the bar unobtrusively playing with a stir-stick when I arrive. The furniture in the bar is innocuous but pleasantly contemporary, cool grays and blues in typical modernist style. The lounge is airy, comfortable, with the new type of bar that opens on the world with tall windows and a real view, unlike the old, dark, windowless, closed-in drinking places of the past. I look for the bandstand, for a piano that Diana might have played, but there is nothing there to tell me that music was ever played in this lounge, apart from the only decoration in the bar, a colorful screen, depicting musical instruments in an abstract modernist arrangement — scarlet, blue, yellow, painted and lacquered on smooth blond wood, a guitar, percussion instruments. I wonder where the screen might have come from, whether it might have been handmade by some local Island craftsperson. It's beautiful, well-made, a one-of-a-kind object.

The nametag on the bartender's white blouse tells me her name is Lisa. She is a typical Vancouver Island young woman, pretty and blond. She hasn't made any special attempt to make herself look anything else but cleanly-dressed, neat, modestly well-turned out. She has green eyes with long lashes, a straight nose and the straight-speaking manner common to Vancouver Island women, Diana included. Yes, she allows, when I ask her, she knows who Diana is. In fact, she went to school with her at Nanaimo District Secondary School, about 20 years ago, and knew who Diana was even then, though she didn't know Diana well. "She was a year or two ahead of me," Lisa says. "People talked about her because she played music. Everyone in school knew who she was." As our talk proceeds, Lisa helps me to correct a mistaken belief that Diana had once attended Dover Bay High School. My wife and I had traveled to the edge of town to view the school, thinking that Diana had spent time there. "It wasn't even *open* in those days," Lisa insists. "The only school that Diana attended was the same one I did, the Nanaimo District Secondary School."

She tells me she never worked on the nights that Diana played at the Coast Bastion, so she never got to know her very well. She says a fellow worker in the back might know more about Diana. Without being asked, she leaves me at the counter to fetch Faye. Faye speaks in a matter-of-fact way. "I didn't know her very well. I only used to see her here sometimes. Some of the others knew her better than me, used to hang around with her a little bit. She was a really nice girl, though. Quiet."

"Yeah, quiet," says Lisa, "and friendly. Didn't you find her friendly, Faye?"

"Yeah, but mostly quiet. If you like, you can come in tomorrow and talk to Gail and Lorrie, they knew her much better than we did."

Faye says that Diana sometimes comes back to the hotel to visit the other bartenders who were her friends, though she also lets me know that Diana doesn't play at the Coast Bastion any more, that she's way beyond that now.

"The last time I saw her, last year some time. I think she was here to open up the television station or something," Faye says, "She said she comes back to town a lot to see her mother. Her mom's been sick, I think. I thought that was nice. She's so famous and she's still got time to come home to see her mom. I thought that was nice."

Lisa is looking forward to a long, boring night without many customers. As a way of making conversation, she asks me what I think has made Diana popular. I tell Lisa that Diana has what some people call an "arresting voice," that she is able to get inside a song and tell a story with it, that her presentation of songs is very cool, gives people room to find their own experience within the song. She does every song right to the bottom, as perfectly as she can — the arrangements, the musical breaks, the phrasing. Lisa is barely interested; it's obviously not her kind of music, not her kind of life.

"Well," she says, "she's brought a lot of attention to Nanaimo, anyway."

A propos of the kind of attention Nanaimo is receiving, I tell her about the *Time* magazine writer who wrote that Nanaimo is a suburb of Vancouver.

"They *wish*!" says Lisa in a sudden burst of civic pride that takes me by surprise.

"Well, I suppose we *do* wish it was, in a way," I reply, trying to be the genial Vancouverite, spending the day in Nanaimo, "Nanaimo is a good place to get away to if you live in Vancouver. Not so good to commute from, though. Takes too much time if you have to travel every day."

"So I guess Diana always wanted to get out of Nanaimo to the big city," Lisa says.

"Well, she always speaks well of her hometown, and she comes back here often enough. Every month in fact, according to my information. But she said she always wanted to live some place bigger for the sake of her career."

"Where does she live now?" Lisa asks.

"Mostly in New York. She spends a lot of time in Los Angeles, too. And of course, she's touring in Europe, now."

"Not me," says Lisa, "I've always lived here, always will. There's plenty here for me, enough to keep me going all my life. I don't even like it in Vancouver. Been there once or twice, for concerts and what not when I was younger. The concerts were okay, but I just wanted to come back home, you know. Too noisy. Too crowded. Too much smoke and gas."

No trace of envy for others living elsewhere. She really means it. I've met many other Islanders who feel the same as she does. She would rather be in Nanaimo sitting behind the bar on a Monday night than enjoy all the celebrity that Diana Krall, her famous schoolmate, now enjoys. Her attitude is fairly typical of Nanaimo residents and residents of Vancouver Island in general. It's not at all an absence of curiosity about the world outside the Island, and it's not at all any kind of hostility toward the outside world, either. It's just a simple sense of being frankly in place, with no better place in life to be. If you've lived on the Island, even for the briefest time, you always want to come back to it. Diana has never forgotten Nanaimo, her parents and the people of her hometown. She keeps coming back, too.

Michael Matthews, an old university friend, now a teacher in the English Department at Malaspina University-College, provided me with another take on Diana's place in the history of jazz at the Coast Bastion. He went to interview the bartenders there on my behalf.

The piano bar at the Coast Hotel opened in October, 1985, and a few years later Diana started to play on the baby grand there on Saturday nights. She had already been playing at the NHL restaurant, but couldn't perform in the cocktail lounge until she was of age.

Gail Manz and Lorrie Kean, two of Nanaimo's favorite bartenders, remember how shy and quiet the young Diana was. "Was everything okay?" she would ask, uncertainly, after every performance. "I mean, really okay?"

"The girls really encouraged her," Gail says. "She was a bit shy, and quiet, but so gracious for someone her age, and very anxious to do a good job."

Gail says the piano bar drew "a mixed bag" of people, but there was always a following for Steve Jones, Mike Ocsko, Jackie Droz, and some of the other duos. Diana, too, had a following.

"But Nanaimo is full of good artists and musicians," Gail says, "And Diana was just one of them. I thought she was great, but I never thought she'd be the success she's become. She was just a local kid with lots of talent. We had all kinds of excellent entertainers here, and Diana was just one of them. I expected she'd do well on the local circuit."

"Then, too, we were all into rock and roll then," Lorrie explains, "so we weren't really interested."

Diana's parents were there every Saturday to cheer her on, and she drew a substantial following, playing a mix of standard jazz and classical music. She'd also sing occasionally, but this wasn't encouraged by the management, who preferred to have background piano music only.

Gail describes Diana as an attractive girl who was always dressed in a very casual way. "Nothing too wild. Always tasteful, but not elaborate. She was really a lovely gal, though. It was a treat to have met and have known her. I'm so pleased that we hosted her in our little lounge."

"And she could tickle the ivories like you wouldn't believe," adds Lorrie.

"It's just fantastic to see how well she is doing now," Gail says, "because she really worked very hard to get where she is."

Evelyn and Bert Hepinstall are long-time Nanaimo residents and serious jazz buffs.

"We first heard Diana play when she was about 15 years old and playing in the NHL restaurant," Evelyn says. "She looked nervous, and was reading sheet music, but as soon as I heard her I said to Bert, 'We've gotta watch this kid, there's something going on here.' I just really liked her sounds."

The next time they heard Diana she was playing at the Coast, and they liked her even more. Evelyn and Bert also heard Diana play at Chez Michel and remember an occasion when Diana, quite nervous, had to perform against a lot of racket from a group of professional people who were drinking and noisy. "She had to really pay her dues, playing at some of these places," Evelyn recalls. "I don't remember her singing in those days, it's was just piano as far I was recall. I wondered if maybe she was encouraged to sing the way so many women jazz pianists are. Men can just play, but women are always encouraged to sing."

Evelyn also remembers the company Diana kept. "There were a lot of good musicians playing at Tio's Restaurant in Nanaimo in those days. I think she would have met John Clayton and Jeff Hamilton and maybe Bud Shank when she played there. Her father would have met those people when he dined there, and I think he introduced Diana to him. John Clayton was something of a 'big brother' to Diana when she started to look across the border for what she could do next. There's no question that who you meet makes a big difference. And I think her teacher, Jimmy Rowles, was a big factor in deciding where Diana should go and what she should do. He was very influential in L.A. in those days."

"Do we still go to hear Diana? You bet we do!" Evelyn exclaims. "We hear her anytime she's in the area, and have even gone as far as to Portland's Schnitzer Concert Hall to hear her perform there."

———

The posters in front of the Queen's advertise an impressive list of some of the most popular musicians to come out of this part of the country and make a name for themselves outside of British Columbia. Bif Naked, a latter-day punk rocker, currently enjoying a burst of fame on the strength of a recent album, is advertised as the act for the following week. Allison Crowe, a jazz pianist and singer from Victoria inspired by Diana's example, appeared here some time earlier, and the poster advertising her engagement still remains. Barney Bentall, a much-admired folk-rock artist based in

Vancouver, appeared the week before.

The room inside the Queen's is surprisingly small given that some of the acts advertised outside would draw as many as a thousand people in Vancouver. There is room for about 100 people standing room only inside the Queen's. It's a dark, small room with brick walls and wooden pillars, redolent with smells of tobacco smoke from the last generation. The no-smoking rule enforced in many B.C. drinking establishments is not enforced here. The parts of the room that aren't red brick are painted flat black.

There are photographs in frames on the walls and pillars, men with guitars, presumably blues artists past and present. I recognize the picture of Jim Byrne, a popular Vancouver-based blues and television performer. Another photo looks like Canadian blues player Colin James, often based in Vancouver, and there is a picture of John Hammond, the man who discovered and produced so many jazz and blues musicians. The others are unnamed black men alone with their guitars or standing in groups beside trains in railroad stations. There's nothing on the pictures to identify them or to suggest that they have actually played the Queen's. Some of the photos are obviously from the 1940s and 1950s, pictures of blues players whose names are long forgotten, commemorated here in Nanaimo, where the blues has a long tradition and is still widely played by many Island bands. Evelyn Hepinstall later informs me that many of the people shown on the photographs actually used to play one-night stands in the Queen's. She remembers seeing John Hammond, Junior Wells, Duke Robillard, the Dirty Dozen Zydeco Band, and thinks they might have been brought over to the Island through a pipeline connected to the Yale Hotel in Vancouver, but she's not sure.

It's early in the evening, but the music has already started. A piano-less quartet is wailing away on stage, led by a tall gray-haired saxophonist, the oldest member of the group in his forties, accompanied on bass by a younger man in a black sports jacket in his late thirties. I later learn that these two men are clinicians hired by the college to assist the young musicians, helping them to find their way into playing these tunes and offering advice on their performances. The catalog for the Music Department at the college says that the students will be required to perform publicly four or five times in the course of their program of study, and I presume this is one of those occasions.

There are only two tables occupied, by students waiting to play in the jam. Two men and a woman well past the first years of their middle-age, obviously regulars, are sitting together at the bar, drinking and smoking. They're mostly indifferent to the music. Several other younger people are very much interested and turn in their bar chairs to pay closer attention to what is happening on stage. These musicians are earnest.

The quartet makes its way through a repertoire of standards: *Autumn Leaves; East of the Sun, West Of The Moon; This Must Be Love.* The older musician picks up a soprano sax to play the samba theme from the movie *Black Orpheus.* Listening to these old standards amidst the dark and smoke-smelling atmosphere provides a nostalgic pleasure. There is a young trombonist, wearing a bright red sweater, bright blue pants, a blue and red baseball hat, who looks like Leonardo di Caprio or a young Chet Baker, and rarely leaves the stage, playing every tune. As the night wears on, new young musicians arrive. Two studious looking young women arrive carrying their fat copies of *The New Real Book*, instrument cases in tow. By 10:30 p.m. there are six musicians on stage, some of them barely old enough to be allowed in the bar, and another six or eight fingering their instruments offstage, waiting to be heard. Each of the musicians takes a turn on stage and plays a solo. A young woman shyly plays part of a duet on the Dizzy Gillespie classic, *Night In Tunisia*, lyrically, though without much power, making what I think are a few small slips in intonation and melody, but plays credibly, with real emotion. A tall blond saxophonist makes his way through a solo very smoothly and competently, but apparently doesn't want to play more and leaves the stage for the night, though I would have liked to have heard more of his playing. The two young women with their *New Real Books* also have a go. The taller one plays electric piano, the other plays saxophone.

They're all having fun, even though they are being graded and judged on their performances.

By midnight, most of the musicians are packing up their instruments, though the two clinicians keep playing until the last. The water around Nanaimo does seem to be infused with jazz. Inspired by the dedicated teachers at Malaspina University-College and by the success of Diana Krall and Ingrid Jensen, the music students of Nanaimo have happily found their way to jazz, and they are playing it with all their hearts.

———

Jazz has always had a following on Canada's west coast, particularly in Vancouver, the largest city on the coast. The first jazz artists that I remember in Vancouver were swing or mainstream musicians who played dance music in the nightclubs and gigs at dance halls and high-school graduations throughout the 1940s and 1950s. Big band swing in Vancouver is associated with the names of several bandleaders — Dal Richards, Fraser McPherson, Dave Robbins, and Lance Harrison. The Dal Richards Orchestra played at the Panorama Roof of the Hotel Vancouver for 25 years, the longest running dance band engagement in Canadian history. During that time, 'The Band at the Top of the Town', as it became known, was featured on over 2000 coast-to-coast broadcasts on CBC Radio. Other bands played at Isy's and the Cave, two legendary nightclubs, and members of these bands played Sunday night concerts during the 1950s at the Georgia Auditorium about once a month.

Aficionados of the bebop revolution hung out at a club in an alley behind the gym of Canada's strong man, the weightlifter and professional wrestler Doug Hepburn. The club was called the Cellar, consistent with its damp unlighted ambience, its cold cement floors and low ceilings. Bryan Stovell, who later became Diana Krall's high-school band teacher, was sometimes heard playing his bass in the Cellar. The Cellar routinely featured some the greatest jazz musicians of the age. Art Pepper, a passionate and intelligent alto-saxophonist, was one visitor, and so was the Los Angeles tenor player Harold Land. Trumpeter Joe Gordon played a two-week gig at the Cellar, and the Charles Mingus band, featuring drummer Danny Richmond and trumpeter Lonny Hillier, were headliners in a remarkable series of shows in 1961, in which Mingus fought verbal and sometimes actual physical battles with patrons who would not agree to a reduce their noise and laughter during the band's performances. During another show at the Flat Five on Broadway, Mingus, filled with self-hatred, frustration, and rage at the tail-end of a road trip, deliberately lacerated the thumb on his right hand from tip to knuckle on the jagged edge of a sardine can while on stage, and then announced to the horrified audience, "That's it for this gig."

The Cellar was run under the auspices of a non-profit organization headed by saxophonist Dave Quarin. The house band was led by pianist Al Neil, who during the late 1950s played bebop heavily influenced by Thelonious Monk and Bud Powell, but whose musical interest and ravenous artistic curiosity soon enough led him far beyond these bebop beginnings. Neil is still justifiably remembered as a kind of local genius, for his wide-ranging activities in other performance arts as much as for his contributions to the jazz scene. There are many active musicians not only in Vancouver, but across the country today, who readily own that Neil taught them all the basics of music when they played with him at the Cellar during the late 1950s and early 1960s. Neil is the musician of record on one of the first and best jazz and poetry collaborations ever made. The LP KENNETH PATCHEN READS WITH JAZZ IN CANADA is still available from Folkways Records, featuring Neil and alto-saxophonist Dale Hillary accompanying the American proto-beat poet. Neil has written a semi-documentary memoir called *Changes*, detailing his life as a jazz pianist and the lives of associated musicians trying to make a living in the unsympathetic environment of Vancouver at the time.

Always a restlessly creative personality, Al Neil was influenced not only by Charlie Parker, Thelonious Monk, and other heroes of modern jazz, but also by the dadaist movement in art. Consistent with his dadaist convictions, he never allowed himself to settle into any kind of fixed artistic or musical groove, and soon enough outgrew his acolytes, moving toward the outer reaches of the jazz experience, becoming more and more avant garde in his approach. His performances became so "outside" that the other musicians found they could no longer work with him. For a few years after his tour of duty at the Cellar, Neil was musically inactive, but in the middle '60s, a small group of younger musicians fresh out of high school sought him out and founded a new trio with Neil as the leader. They set up the Sound Gallery on Fourth Avenue to support a wide variety of artistic adventures.

The work of the Al Neil trio, featuring drummer Gregg Simpson and bassist Rick Anstey, is still an example of some of the most "out there" avant garde music ever played. The quality of this music bears comparison to the likes of Cecil Taylor, Sun Ra, Albert Ayler, and others who have taken jazz far beyond conventional melodies, harmonies, rhythms, and even beyond what most would consider music, embracing noise itself and chance productions of sound and silence in the manner of the master of aleatoric music, John Cage. Together with his wife, Marguerite, who played the violin, Neil entered another musical arena, touring Canadian cities from time to time, performing an outrageous mix of dada music and performance art to university audiences and the downtown arts crowds. An Al Neil musical performance typically involved dadaist instruments of made of tin-cans, blocks of wood, strings with bells, bicycle horns, coal-buckets, tar-colored ropes, bottle caps, plastic rejectamenta of various types, the parts of broken dolls, wires strung in various ways, glass floats and other fishing paraphernalia cast up by the tide outside his home in Dollarton, half a mile from the site of the shack where famed modernist author Malcolm Lowry lived and wrote.

Before he moved on to these beyond-the-border styles of music and art, Neil inspired a cadre of jazz musicians who are still important on the Canadian jazz scene. Juno Award winner P.J. Perry, one of the best alto-saxophonists ever to come out of Vancouver, credits his early education to Al Neil's influence, as does Don Thompson, one of the most highly respected of all Canadian jazz musicians. Jerry Fuller, another Al Neil band member, was often heard drumming behind Don Thompson's bass while backing visiting American jazz musicians at the well-known Toronto jazz venues at the Bourbon Street Jazz Club and George's Spaghetti House in Toronto during the 1970s and 1980s. Don Thompson became one of Diana Krall's champions and mentors while she was living in Toronto.

During these years you could hear Dizzy Gillespie play with the Lalo Schiffren Orchestra in the downtown Queen Elizabeth Playhouse, the quintet of Miles Davis and the Mastersounds featuring Wes Montgomery at the Inquisition. Later, Philly Jo Jones appeared at the Flat Five on Broadway, fresh from his participation on Milestones, a centrally important record in the development of the classical Miles Davis Quintet featuring Jones, John Coltrane, and Cannonball Adderley. Jones played drums behind a local band featuring Vancouver trumpet sensation Ron Proby. Other clubs came and went — The Black Spot, where young musicians, some of them active in the University of British Columbia Jazz Society, played every night of the week in different combinations, the Den, Goof's Pad, the Flat Five, and the Blue Note on Broadway. Throughout the 1970s and part of the 1980s, local jazz musicians played gigs in restaurants like Carnegie's and went to the Classical Joint in Vancouver's Gastown to jam. June Katz, an expatriate jazz singer from New York, opened a restaurant called the Alma Cafe near to the University of British Columbia campus. The Hugh Fraser Band, featuring the Cannonball Adderley acolyte, Campbell Ryga, the son of author George Ryga, often appears there.

Today, Vancouver continues to support a handful of restaurants and clubs which feature mainstream jazz. Kenny Coleman, an excellent crooner from the Frank Sinatra, Tony Bennett, and Mel Torme school is a regular at the downtown supper club called the Cave. Linton Garner, the brother of the late piano great Erroll Garner, strokes the keys nightly as the house pianist at Rossini's just across the street from Kitsilano Beach. The downtown Railway Club is primarily a venue for rising rock and roll performers, but jazz-oriented musicians like Veda Hille, a song-writer and piano player often accompanied by jazz cellist Peggy Lee, and a rising new pianist-singer from Vancouver Island, Allison Crowe, are sometimes heard there, too. Lee Aaron, a one-time hard-rocker, appears weekend nights at the Rusty Gull in North Vancouver, singing jazz standards, amidst huge photographs of the ship-building history of North Vancouver mixed with classic photos of the greats of jazz: Billie Holiday, John Coltrane, Louis Armstrong, Miles Davis, Dexter Gordon, Charlie Haden, Dizzy Gillespie, and Charlie Parker. Young mainstream musicians like the trumpeter Jeff Mahoney make their money by playing aboard the cruise ships departing from Vancouver in the summertime.

In the late 1980s, a dedicated coterie of avant-garde jazz musicians established a base camp at the club known as the Glass Slipper on 11th Avenue two blocks away from the location of the older Cellar, and then moved a couple of streets away to inhabit an old revivalist church hall behind the Biltmore Hotel on Kingsway. On any given night, a visitor to the Slipper could hear the avant garde jazz stylings of the marvelous internationally recognized reed-player, bandleader, and composer from Quebec, Francois Houle, surrounded by award-winning musicians like trombonist Brad Muirhead, drummer Dylan van der Schyff, guitarist Tony Wilson, cellist Peggy Lee, trumpeter John Korsrud with saxophonist Coat Cooke and their Hard Rubber Orchestra. I have given poetry readings there accompanied by the Henry Boudin Trio and Coat Cooke. Campbell Ryga, Phil Dwyer, Ross Taggart, Oliver Gannon, and Bruno Hubert now appear regularly at a new, upscale basement restaurant club called the Cellar, no doubt named in memory of the distinctly downscale club in the alley at Main and Broadway.

Since 1985, the West Coast jazz scene has been enlivened by the duMaurier Vancouver International Jazz Festival. Once every year at the end of June the city hosts contingents of jazz musicians from the United States, Europe, Latin American, and Africa. The Festival, sponsored by the Coastal Jazz and Blues Society, headed by artistic director Ken Pickering, is the major event of the Vancouver jazz calendar. The thousands of concerts the Coastal Jazz and Blues Society has presented throughout its history include notable performances by Miles Davis, Sun Ra, Clusone Trio, Shirley Horn, Dave Douglas, Ornette Coleman, Marilyn Crispell, Enrico Rava, Dizzy Gillespie, John Zorn, Evan Parker, Sonny Rollins, Cecil Taylor, Gilberto Gil, Wynton Marsalis, London Jazz Composers Orchestra, Vienna Art Orchestra, Johnny Griffin, Steve Lacy, New Orchestra Workshop, Chick Corea, Eugene Chadbourne, ICP Orchestra, Christy Doran, Kazutoki Umezu, Youssou NDour, Louise Sclavis, Georg Graewe, Carmen McRae, Lol Coxhill, Carol Sloane, Paul Plimley, Jay McShann, Bill Frisell, Jane Bunnett, Ken Vandermark, Oliver Jones, Medeski Martin and Wood, Francoise Houle, Jackie McLean, Otis Rush, Cyrus Chestnut, Charles Gayle, John Tchicai, Joe Henderson, Joe Pass, Rene Lussier, ROVA, Tony Williams, Horace Tapscott, Carla Bley, George Gruntz, Joe McPhee, Don Byron, Pat Metheny, Fred Van Hove, Justine, Barry Elmes, Dave Brubeck, Guillermo Gregorio . . . "From ragtime to no time, from the blues to world music traditions and beyond," the advertisements for the Festival declare, "the widest spectrum is represented in our presentations. This list is just the tip of the iceberg . . ."

The festival opens with a free afternoon event in Gastown, featuring two stages and half a dozen different acts. There are free concerts every day on Granville Island, under the shadow of the Granville Bridge. The last two days of the Festival are always given over to a series of concerts and workshops held on the green playing field of Roundhouse Park and in the rooms of the Roundhouse Cultural Centre, a rambling building converted from a railroad roundhouse.

At night, more than a dozen cafes, restaurants, and clubs feature bands and individual players from every country playing every type of jazz and world music. Two theatres, the Vogue and the Orpheum, feature big-time jazz names, and lesser-known stars can be heard at the East Vancouver Cultural Centre. Local musicians are inspired by the opportunity to play together with visiting musicians, both as headliners and as back-up musicians. Local drummers and bassists are particularly busy — the drummer Dylan van der Schyff one year played no fewer than 22 gigs in a five day period, hauling his drum kit from place to place without losing a beat, to the great admiration of all his peers. The light summer is saturated with the sound of horns and beating drums.

The Vancouver International Jazz Festival has become a key venue in the international jazz festival circuit, which has become the main staging ground for jazz in the last two decades. Diana Krall has been no stranger to this stage. In the liner notes to her album ALL FOR YOU, Diana thanks the people who have been important in her life and given support to her career. Among those acknowledged are famous musicians, former manager Mary Ann Topper, the musicians and the technical crew on her record, publicists, former teachers like Louise Rose and Bryan Stovell, the Horner family in Nanaimo, and her own family, Jim, Adella, and Michelle Krall. But she singles out for attention, "My friends at duMaurier Jazz — Ken Pickering; Daryl Mar; Marc Vasey; Dave Sherman." During the 1990s, Diana performed every year at the festival for five years running.

The festival is administered entirely by the Coastal Jazz and Blues Society, founded 17 years ago by its present Artistic Director, Ken Pickering, and a small crowd of his friends. In spite of the growth of the festival, the Coastal Jazz and Blues Society remains, to say the least, a very compact organization, with probably no more than five or six full-time employees who carry the heavy task of running the event, aided by hundreds of volunteers, ushers, door stewards, drivers, concession operators, mc's, sound and amplification experts, ready to give their time for the benefit of the festival, the performers, and the fans. Society member John Orysik took the time from his busy schedule to reminisce about one of the festival's greatest successes and one of its most popular stars, Diana Krall.

John recalls Diana playing a free concert on Granville Island with her trio on a bill that also featured the fine veteran Vancouver saxophonist and bandleader, Fraser MacPherson. MacPherson is the only other Canadian jazz musician besides Oscar Peterson to be honored as a Member of the Order of Canada on the strength of his lifetime contributions to music. The young Diana was in awe that she could be considered worthy to be spoken of in the same breath, John explains. "She came from humble beginnings," he says, "she had a lot of humility, and she always dedicated herself to achieving success through paying attention to musical values above all else." This public concert on Granville Island was followed by a series of gigs at different Vancouver clubs and restaurants — the Alma Street Café, the Blue Note, and Django's.

At subsequent festivals, Artistic Director Ken Pickering presented Diana Krall to an increasingly wider audience. "We recognized her talent right from the beginning," John Orysik notes, and "we've done everything we can to support her and make sure she obtains the recognition she deserves. We knew from the beginning that she was great, from the audience reactions. Other artists said she could go far, and we believed that." Pickering also made representations to other jazz festival organizers to include Diana on their bill.

When Diana appeared at the festival in June 1992, Pickering made sure that she opened the show at the Vancouver East Cultural Centre, with Oliver Jones as headliner. Her first recording was still a full year from its release at the time, but the Vancouver jazz audience woke up at this concert to this home-grown talent, Orysik recalls. In June 1996, she appeared at the Orpheum, Vancouver's largest and most luxurious theatre, as the opening act for piano legend George Shearing. Two years later, Diana Krall and her trio were the headline act for the festival. The concert was sold out months in advance, and the same is true of every other Diana Krall concert held in Vancouver since.

Although many sources report that Diana received a grant from the Vancouver International Jazz Festival in 1981 to study at the Berklee College of Music in Boston, Bryan Stovell, her music teacher at the time and himself a Berklee alumnus, suggests that the grant came instead from the organizers of a jazz festival in the nearby town of New Westminster in recognition of her prodigious talent, supplemented by a bursary from Berklee for $2,500. Regardless of the source of this support, Diana Krall's career as a professional jazz artist was launched when she ventured to Boston.

The Education of Diana **K**rall

In his modest way, Bryan Stovell takes only a little credit for Diana Krall's decision to attend the Berklee College of Music in Boston, which he himself attended in the 1970s. Perhaps his stories of life at Berklee and what he learned there influenced Diana's choice. When she graduated from Nanaimo and District Secondary School in the spring of 1982, Diana made plans to travel east to Boston to attend Berklee, aided by scholarships she had won traveling to Canadian cities, chaperoned by Bryan Stovell.

Bryan Stovell, a music teacher at the Nanaimo District Secondary School, was flipping through the channels on television one night when he chanced upon a local cable television clip of Diana playing with a band under the leadership of the well-known local Woodlands Junior Secondary School bandleader, Dave Strong. Diana may have been as young as 14 years old. The band was playing a blues tune, possibly *Night Train*, Stovell recalls.

Stovell was an experienced jazz player who earned his chops during the early '60s in Vancouver. He grew up in the resort town of Qualicum Beach, a few miles north of Nanaimo, where he taught himself how to play the clarinet by listening to Dixieland recordings and the music of the Benny Goodman bands. The son of emigrants from England, Stovell says he didn't learn to read music until he went to the University of British Columbia music school. He trained at the University of British Columbia to become an elementary school teacher in 1958 and 1959, then taught English, social studies, and "some music" to elementary students at Harewood School in Nanaimo for two years, before returning to the UBC to upgrade his teaching credentials. There he began to expand his formal music education.

During these years, he took up the bass on the advice of a more experienced musician friend, John Capon, who told him that bass players are always in demand. Stovell played with some of the big bands around town, primarily the house band at the Vancouver Hotel, and he also met a group of up-and-coming young musicians studying in the Music Department at UBC. These musicians were also playing gigs in some of the city's clubs — the Cellar, the Black Spot, the Inquisition, and the Flat Five. Stovell says with some pride ("and a little irony," he adds) that he played bass with the group that was playing on the very night that the Cellar was finally closed. His musical friends in Vancouver included trombonist John Capon, drummer Terry Clarke, bassist Don Thompson, trumpeter Don Clark, and trombonist Ian McDougall from the internationally renowned Canadian Boss Brass — a literal 'who's who' of some of the finest active Canadian jazz musicians today.

Stovell remembers a meeting of some of the members of this tight-knit group of young local musicians in Vancouver sometime around 1967, when they got together to discuss the possibility of testing their musical talents in the deeper waters of Toronto, closer to the international jazz scene. Don Thompson, in particular, urged him to join the exodus —"Come on, man, you can make it!" Because he was married and owed a responsibility to his wife and family (and "because Don's awesome talent scared the hell out of me," he adds), Stovell decided to stick it out in Nanaimo. By 1970, he was teaching in the Wellington Junior Secondary School, then later taught at a school in the Departure Bay area of Nanaimo, finally settling into a job as music teacher at the Nanaimo and District Secondary School, acting as bandleader to Grade 11 and 12 students there.

Stovell remembers that night when he first saw Diana Krall on television as an important moment in his life. "Two or three bars into the tune," he says, "I said to myself: 'What's that?' And it was Diana." As he recalls, at that moment he felt like a "basketball coach who'd just seen a seven-foot-tall kid in the hallway who was co-ordinated." His enthusiasm for Diana overwhelmed him: "This is super-talented. This is special, it belongs to the world . . . Well, more than Nanaimo, anyway." Diana would soon leave Junior Secondary School to attend his school. Stovell says he felt the immediate sense that he had to begin to prepare for her arrival. "I felt a far greater sense of responsibility, because I have a great reverence for the music. This was special. It would be like a science teacher who uncovered an Einstein. To me it was that big." He remembers his awe at the rhythmic sense the girl possessed, which he recognized as coming out of the piano stylings of Oscar Peterson. "Anyone who's in jazz knows to look for that special sense of timing and swing," he explains. "It's subtle, but when someone has it, you know it. Diana unquestionably had it."

When he learned that her name was Diana Krall, he remembered that he had attended high school with Jim Krall and that Jim Krall had married Adella Wende, another classmate. He was sure that Diana Krall must be their daughter, and although he had lost contact with them over the years, he decided to give them a call.

"I've gotta talk about your daughter," he said to Adella on the telephone.

"Oh," said Adella, "what's she done wrong?"

Stovell told her without reserve his amazement at Diana's abilities. He told Adella that he was convinced she was definitely capable of a strong career in jazz or popular music.

"That's nice of you to say," Adella replied, full of doubt about a future career for Diana playing in bars and hanging around with possibly disreputable jazz musicians, "but Diana's going to university." At that time, Diana's parents, for all their real love for her, really had no inkling of the immensity of their daughter's talent, or that she was anything other than a normally intelligent junior high-school student, bound for a secure and normal professional career like theirs.

Stovell lost no time in beginning the task of educating his newfound prodigy. Even before she began to attend Stovell's high school, he gave her some of her first recordings of contemporary modern jazz. She had already heard Fats Waller and some of the other classical boogie-woogie and stride pianists beloved by Jim Krall, as well as some of the classical swing pianists — Nat Cole, for one, and Oscar Peterson. Stovell made sure she had the opportunity to hear the best of contemporary jazz at the time. He gave her Bill Evans' WALTZ FOR DEBBY and LIVE AT THE VILLAGE VANGUARD; he made sure she had access to Charlie Parker and John Coltrane, Carmen McRae and Sarah Vaughan.

Throughout the following months and years, Diana would often visit Bryan Stovell's home and come away carrying a load of LPs to listen to at home. "I already had Miles Davis KIND OF BLUE: it was my only jazz record," Diana recalls. "Then I practiced with the records all the time — the swing of Wynton Kelly on KIND OF BLUE, Ahmad Jamal for the use of space, Bill Evans for harmony, some of Keith Jarrett, too."

When Diana entered Nanaimo District Secondary School, she was involved immediately in the school's concert band, which had a classical focus. She was assigned a role as third clarinet in the concert band, a place far beneath her actual musical talent, Stovell recalls, but it was part of the discipline of musical training in the school. Participation in the concert band was compulsory, and every music student had to take the place they were assigned. "She was a great kid," Stovell says, "and she did it because that was the kind of kid she was, and she did it happily. She never missed a rehearsal, she was on the spot for every performance, and she was always ready to help the other kids in the band." Stovell says she was a good student and participated widely in other activities besides music. His one complaint: "she would borrow my reeds and leave lipstick on them."

The keener students in Stovell's classes were encouraged to

join the 18-piece jazz band. Diana eagerly joined the band as its piano player and its main instrumental leader. She also participated in what Stovell calls "spin-off" trios and quartets, which were voluntary because they were extracurricular. Stovell recalls that the other kids were well aware of her superior talents, but her attitude was such that she never became separated from them. The others saw how willingly she accepted the discipline of the position she was assigned in the concert band. They admired her for it. Diana never showed any signs of playing the part of the temperamental prima donna. She was always on time for rehearsals, never put on any airs, showed up smiling and ready for all the collective activities of all the bands. Her enthusiasm for musical activities was so great that on top of the work in the concert band, the jazz band, and the spin-off trios and quartets, she herself organized a Dixieland combo, which the other kids joined enthusiastically. As Diana remarked in an interview in the *Toronto Star*, "I was . . . listening to Elton John, Billy Joel, Supertramp and Peter Frampton . . . I could play all that. But it was the Oscar Peterson Trio and Ed Thigpen and Ray Brown who taught me how to swing, how to improvise." Stovell adds that Diana was "always interested in a wide variety of styles, including what the 'Jazz Police' might consider mouldy-old fig music."

Others were inspired by Diana's example to reach for higher accomplishments. Stovell says that Ingrid Jensen, for one, watched Diana winning recognition for her accomplishments and resolved to do the same. Jensen has subsequently been lauded for her trumpet playing by two of the finest trumpeters in modern jazz, Art Farmer and Clark Terry. Responding to Jensen's first album HIGHER GROUNDS, Farmer has remarked, "Ingrid Jensen's debut album is for sure a most impressive one. Her playing contains all of the elements in rich detail that make this music so loved. Such as feeling, swing, drive, taste, grace and lyricism." Jensen, whose album VERNAL FIELDS was honored with a Canadian Juno Award as Best Mainstream Album of the Year in 1995, acknowledges that Diana's piano playing in school ensembles made a huge impression on her. The two musicians have appeared together on a Fifth Estate Canadian Broadcasting Corporation television special.

Bryan Stovell also instigated the first recording sessions for Diana, working with Scott Littlejohn at his small studio in Nanaimo. The demo tapes produced by Littlejohn were presented to Nanaimo club owners as part of her resume in obtaining jobs. Her first professional audition was in the NHL restaurant, owned by former National Hockey League referee, Lloyd Gilmour. With her always-ready humor, Diana remarks on the appropriateness of a venue connected with the 'NHL' as a good place for the first professional gig of a Canadian jazz pianist. She also worked at the Chez Michel restaurant, owned by Grant Simpson, who now organizes a Gay Nineties Review in Whitehorse in the Yukon Territory. Stovell recalls that the Chez Michel, which also featured some of the best restaurant food in town, catered to an "up-scale" crowd of Nanaimo professional people and others who had at least a passing interest in jazz music. Simpson also brought in a number of stride pianists and other jazz musicians. At Chez Michel, Diana later met Ray Brown for the first time. Another restaurant called Tio's, owned by a Vietnamese immigrant, also featured in some important jazz musicians. Stovell remembers seeing Don Thompson and Terry Clarke playing there behind the great jazz guitarist, Jim Hall. Diana and the other young Nanaimo musicians gained tremendously from the interactions they enjoyed with these visiting musicians. "The musicians were all friends, so the kids had the benefit of all this interaction. It was a great breeding ground for musical accomplishments," Stovell recalls.

During those days, Diana's interest was focused mainly on piano-playing, Bryan Stovell remarks. She loved to sing, though, and when he would drive her to school, they often sang standards together in the car. They would play musical games, too, as part of the musical education process. Stovell would sing a fragment of a line from a song, leaving Diana to pick up the rest of the line. Stovell's line "Set 'em up . . ." would be followed by Diana chiming in with "Joe." "But she was to shy to sing in public," Stovell says. "She thought people would laugh at her."

Bryan Stovell admits that he felt a huge responsibility to ensure that Diana's talent received the widest possible exposure. In order to do that, he remarks, "I knew I had to get her out of the Nanaimo venue. She's bigger than me," he remembers thinking at the time. "I've got to get her out to some of these heavies." He organized to chaperone Diana to music festivals within the province of British Columbia and as far away as the eastern Canadian cities of Hamilton and Toronto. He remembers traveling with her to the New Westminster High School Jazz Festival, which was also attended by jazz groups from the United States, "big names from L.A. and New York," who acted as adjudicators. Stovell believes that her participation in this festival opened up the possibility for her to receive her first music scholarship, which allowed her to travel to the Berklee School of Music in Boston to study piano improvisation. Stovell says his own influence may have been important in encouraging Diana to chose Berklee as the place for her to study: he himself took a "kind of sabbatical" in 1975 and 1976 to attend Berklee. He wanted to "recharge his batteries" away from the somewhat "insular" musical atmosphere of Nanaimo. The broader view of the world he developed there was very useful in terms of being able to give Diana assistance.

In 1981, Stovell traveled with Diana to MusicFest Canada, an invitational festival attended by the cream of the crop from festivals all over the country, held that year in Hamilton, Ontario. The occasion was adjudicated by the famed Canadian bandleader Phil Nimmons and also by the Edmonton pianist Tommy Banks, recently appointed (in 2000) to the Canadian Senate for his lifelong achievements in music and entertainment.

While in Hamilton, Stovell reconnected with the trombonist John Capon, with whom he had worked in Vancouver during the early '60s at the University of British Columbia. Capon immediately suggested that the two of them should make their way from Hamilton to Toronto where a music clinic was being organized around the Phil Nimmons big band. Capon was a member of this band, along with another of Stovell's old companions from

Vancouver, the bassist Don Thompson. Stovell says that Diana jumped at the chance to practice with these heavyweight Canadian musicians, and the two of them spent a week in Toronto, playing music with some of the best jazz musicians in the country.

Stovell recalls an amusing incident involving Don Thompson on the first occasion he met Diana. Stovell asked Thompson if he might provide some lessons to his young student. Thompson allowed that he was very busy with a host of other musical projects; still, he sometimes took on particularly able and talented students, and in order to determine if Diana measured up to his standards, he would have to put her to a test. "Bring her over to the house," Thompson told Stovell, "and I'll check her out."

Storyteller Stovell reports the dialog. "Turn around and I'm going to play a chord voicing," Thompson told Diana. "See if you can reproduce it." He then played what Stovell describes as very complicated chord voicing. Diana went to the piano and reproduced it perfectly. "OK," said Thompson, "I think I can work with you." This was Diana's first encounter with Thompson as a teacher and mentor. Their student-mentor relationship would be taken up again in the late 1980s when Diana moved to Toronto to play professional gigs.

Stovell's memory is not entirely exact on the question of the year in which he again chaperoned Diana to MusicFest in Toronto — according to his best memory it was either 1982 or 1983. Shane Fawkes, another Stovell student, who usually played bass in Diana's trio, had graduated, and was not available to accompany the trio that year, and Stovell himself filled in playing bass. Accompanied by Stovell, Diana won a silver medal at the event, second place for all of Canada.

With his characteristic modesty, Bryan Stovell claims that he hardly taught Diana anything at all: "To tell you the truth, I didn't teach her anything. She got it straight off the records, and it came off her fingers." He does take credit for teaching her one thing: "She was 16 or 17, flittering all over the place," and in her youthful excitement, she couldn't always remember the names and the order of the tunes she was planning to play on her gigs. "I told her to 'Get a list' — swing tunes on one list, ballads on another so we weren't mucking around and figuring out what to do." During a recent performance, he noticed that Diana still reaches into her pocket and pulls out a list of tunes to place on the piano before beginning her performances. "So I can take credit for that," he says. For her part, Diana says, "Bryan turned me on to Bill Evans, and how to play trio." Important lessons, indeed.

Stovell's influence on the young pianist didn't stop there, either. He was also probably actively helpful in making the introductions required to allow Diana to take on her first professional musical engagements in her own home town. Bryan Stovell was present throughout Diana's high-school years, providing support, encouragement, and advice, working not only with her in the high-school programs, but connecting her to the music program at Malaspina University-College. Diana herself always mentions his name as a prime influence, thanking him in print on her album covers, acknowledging him among many other more famous personalities who helped her along the way. "Her world went far beyond mine in the '80s," Stovell admits, "and I am very grateful to her for still mentioning me." Throughout Bryan Stovell's 37 years as a music instructor, his home was always open to his students, who came to revere him for his openness and generosity. A friend of mine, who has personally known some of Bryan's students, says that they revere him, like Diana herself, as a "kind of god."

There is no documentary record of the exact time in her life when Diana Krall began to focus her attention on jazz piano, but she likely learned her first jazz in the family home, picking out tunes from the many records of Fats Waller, Oscar Peterson, Nat King Cole, and other jazz pianists in her father's record collection. "I grew up listening to the history of American popular song and jazz, Teddy Wilson, Fats Waller, Duke Ellington, Bing Crosby, Louis Armstrong, since I was a baby," Diana has commented. "My parents, who had very eclectic musical tastes, had cylinder recordings of Billy Murray, Connie Boswell, Helen Kane and others."

The prevailing mythology of jazz strongly suggests that the only true source of this music, down-home authentic jazz, is found in the experience of poverty and humiliation. Ella Fitzgerald grew up in poverty-stricken circumstances, was raised by her mother alone, and suddenly gained a ticket to fame and fortune when she won an amateur contest at the Apollo Theater to sing in the Chick Webb band. Billie Holiday came from the world of bordellos and raunchy nightclubs, where she was expected to earn her money by offering sexual favors to the customers. Louis Armstrong spent part of his youth in a juvenile detention facility in New Orleans. The legendary Bessie Smith, considered the greatest blues artist of all time, was turned away from a hospital after an automobile accident and bled to death without benefit of medical care, only because she was poor and black.

Whether the musicians were born in harsh circumstances or not, the conditions of the 'jazz life' enforced a hard existence on jazz musicians, particularly Afro-American musicians. They faced hard booking schedules, callous and unscrupulous club managers; racist policies in hotels that routinely refused a night's lodging to itinerant black musicians; police who quite routinely arrested entire bands of black musicians, threw them in jail, beat them mercilessly, confiscated their instruments and their vehicles, and sent them back out on the road penniless. The difficulties of the jazz life were compounded by other factors, too: the prevalence of alcoholism, the lack of stable relationships, the presence of organized crime, and the scourge of drug addiction. The number of American jazz musicians who have died young and in humiliating circumstances is legion. Charlie Parker died at the young age of 34, his health irreparably damaged by alcohol and drug abuse. The universally revered Lester Young died at the age of 45 after years of hard travel and racist treatment at the hands of military authorities when he was drafted into the army in World War II and held in an army detention facility. Billie Holiday, exploited by record companies (she never received any

royalties for more than 200 of her recordings), hounded by police, deprived of the right to work because of her drug addiction,
died poor and sick at the age of 44.

There are exceptions to this rule, though, at least in part. Duke
Ellington was raised in Washington in the home of a government
official, where his father was a trusted domestic servant. Duke was
able to establish enough economic independence to buy his own
house in Washington by the time he was 20 years old. The son of a
very successful East St. Louis dentist, Miles Davis died leaving a
personal fortune of $12 million dollars. His early secure economic
circumstances enabled him to move to New York to begin study
at the Juilliard School of Music, although he soon abandoned
Juilliard for the life of a professional musician working in the musical hothouse of New York, where he worked in the band of
Charlie Parker. Yet Davis played the role of the street tough,
which he believed was required as credentials for the authentic
jazz musician.

If a hard life is the only way to win credentials as a serious jazz
artist, Diana Krall entered the jazz world with many strikes
against her. By any measure, the childhood and adolescence of
Diana Krall were completely happy and secure. She never spent a
single day of her young life going without. "I had everything a kid
could want," she says, "including two trips to Disneyland. Yep,
two. My parents have this great relationship."

Diana's parents, like all the other members of their generation,
experienced their childhood in the midst of the upheaval of World
War II, but their later years were lived in the atmosphere of rising
expectations. Post-war prosperity brought with it a growing range
of educational opportunities for the sons and daughters of working
people across the country. For the first time, young people from a
working class background were granted the opportunities to
achieve an education. Many of them took the opportunity to expand their horizons to aim for professional careers. Diana's father,
Jim Krall, became a chartered accountant, who still runs his own
highly successful accountancy business today. Her mother, Adella,
has enjoyed a long career as an extremely popular elementary

school teacher-librarian in Nanaimo. Her uncle, Tom Krall, is a member of the City Council in Nanaimo.

The family may be highly respectable, hard-working, and socially conscientious, but the Kralls are very far from being dull. The prevailing passion of both Jim and Adella Krall has been the love of music of all kinds, from opera and popular ballads to jazz and cowboy songs. Both of them play the piano. Adella sang in a local choir. The home of Diana's maternal grandmother was the scene of weekend dinners where the family and their friends ended up singing songs of every kind around the piano. At these gatherings, her father usually played the piano, and her Aunt Jean, who according to Diana, had a "great voice," usually led the singing. "Typical thing we'd do when I'd go home was to play rummy after dinner and listen to records. My grandmother had a great voice, too. My Aunt Jean had been in vaudeville, my Uncle Andy could sing every national anthem you could throw at him. We'd listen to everything: early American dance bands like Fred Waring's and Jean Goldkette's and lots of classical music from my dad. Creedence Clearwater Revival, choral music, Welsh choirs, hymns, Scottish music. . . . At home, my dad had stacks of old sheet music, this great library of 78s, cylinders, gramophones. Half of the time I didn't know what I was hearing. He'd put a stack of 78s on the record player and play cards. It was his quiet hobby."

A television feature on Diana Krall and her family in Nanaimo broadcast on Bravo's Arts & Minds series adds to this family portrait. Jim Krall, a slim and serious-looking, though unaffected, man, is seated beside Diana's sister, Michelle, in a booth in a small Nanaimo restaurant, chosen because it was a gathering place for the family and their friends during Diana's childhood and youth. "My mom and dad would have a lot of company on a Saturday night and their friends would sit around the piano and sing songs," Jim says. "I don't think that's something that happens any more, unfortunately. It's gone," he concludes, with a touch of regret. "Their house was almost like the neighborhood pub, you know?" Diana says. "That's where everybody convened and had a party and my dad would play the piano and my uncle. They'd turn the light on for people to go home and it would be 6 a.m." During another interview, she remarked, "With the piano we just sang every kind of song. I come from an English-Scottish background so with my grandmother we sang everything from George Formby onwards. I have the tapes of that, where my father played piano and my uncle played accordion and it was a mess. The media have romanticized it, talking about us singing round the family piano, but it wasn't that at all. It was crazy; it was card-playing, it was just like the town pub."

There was more than music in the Krall home. "My dad had a bunch of videos of Jack Benny which we always used to watch," Diana says, noting that some of her favorites were Buster Keaton and the Marx Brothers. "Even though we'd seen them a million times, I'd still laugh like hell whenever I saw them. It's a lesson in timing. Jack Benny's timing was impeccable. It was just a look, but it could be so funny and self-deprecating. You can apply that to anything." A lesson Diana has certainly applied to her music.

Diana would go to her grandparents' home after school and play the piano. "We didn't even know she had a voice in those days," her father says. "I just sang at home," Diana recalls.

In fact, Diana was already seated at the piano stool by the time she was four years old, taking piano lessons from a neighbor, Audrey Thomas. Diana credits her with providing strict and disciplined musical instruction. Audrey Thomas noticed the girl's flair for jazz (inherited from her grandmother, Diana says). At Diana's urging, she would play boogie-woogie pieces over and over again. Diana always tapped her foot loudest to the jazz pieces she was learning to play, though her tastes in music were always varied. "I plucked out *Hey Jude*," Diana says, "and played the *Irish Washerwoman's Boogie* — I think I practiced it to death."

At some time during these years, she also took lessons from Joyce Horner, referred to by the friends who gave me Ms. Horner's name as the "fountainhead of everything" musical in Nanaimo. Joyce Horner's photograph appears in the same gallery of honored Nanaimo cultural figures in the Ports Theatre where Brian

Stovell, Ingrid Jensen, the Nanaimo Concert Band, and Diana herself are similarly honored. Ms. Horner says she taught Diana the basics of music — "You know," she said, "who's who and what's what in music."

"What kind of student would you say she was?" I asked her.

"Oh, she was a very nice girl. Quick learner," Ms. Horner says.

Diana's musical activities were always voluntary. "My father didn't say, 'you have to listen', unless I asked," Diana says. "We'd hang around at breakfast and there'd usually be a jazz record on, and we'd hear it." As she recalls, "Anything my sister and I chose, they never discouraged us. They did have big trust in us. ... My parents always encouraged me to play, but they didn't push me, either. It was a very balanced approach. They said, 'Whatever you want to do, we'll encourage you and support you'." When she was five years old, Diana traveled with her parents to Vancouver to attend a concert by Ella Fitzgerald and Oscar Peterson at the Orpheum Theater. Her mother made a special jacket for her so that she could appear at her best. A black and white photograph in the booklet which accompanies LOVE SCENES depicts a blond and curly-headed tyke of about four or five years old seated smiling happily at the piano stool dressed in her best Sunday frock, commemorating Diana's earliest encounters with musical performance.

Diana's interest in music didn't stop with the piano. Once in Grade IV or Grade V, she tried out for a local youth choir, but she was rejected as a choir member because her voice was already too low! "I auditioned for a soprano," Diana recalls. "The choir director, who was well-meaning, was trying to push my range. I was straining to make these high notes, and getting so stressed. I didn't pass and it just devastated me. I took it personally, like you do at ten. Now, I wish I'd had the confidence to ask to be put at the back with the boys, where I could flirt to my heart's desire and sing tenor." Although she had been rejected by the choir director, choir was still compulsory. Diana adopted a clever stratagem, perhaps to prove to herself and her fellow students her own worth as a music student: "I'd sing out of tune on purpose until he [her teacher] would come with a ruler and say 'Somebody's droning. Somebody's droning.' And the second he would walk by me I would sing perfectly in tune. He could never figure out who did it."

Diana continued to study classical piano into her teenage years, still participating in classical musical recitals at the age of 14, but her interest in jazz was growing. "One day I came home after hanging out with my friends," Diana recalls, "and my dad's standing there, shocked. He goes, 'What the hell are you doing calling Marian McPartland?' I said, 'How'd you know?' ''Cause she just called you back!'"

McPartland was the host of the American radio show *Piano Jazz*. Diana had tracked down her number by calling New York City information. She was looking for a jazz mentor.

———

Louise Rose became a mentor to Diana Krall, teaching her piano improvisation in the early 1980s. Louise was born in Norristown, Pennsylvania, where she grew up in an environment rich with music. By the age of eight, she was already conducting her grandfather's church choir, and as a young adult, she studied musical arranging with no less a figure than Duke Ellington himself, then studied piano improvisation with Oscar Peterson. She also studied with Leonard Bernstein. Sometime in the early 1970s Louise moved to the British Columbia capital of Victoria, where she immediately became deeply involved in the music and arts community. A warm and energetic person, she is an accomplished jazz pianist and recording artist, an ordained Baptist minister, and a dedicated community activist. She is the musical director of the Victoria Good News Choir, and can be seen on television hosting Vision TV's popular *Let's Sing Again*, where she plays piano while leading sing-alongs with Victoria residents. She volunteers her time at several schools in the area, giving her talents freely in the nurturing of young musicians. Her website advertises her as a composer, facilitator, music-maker, pianist, arranger, motivational speaker, and communicator. She is all of that and more.

As a former student of Duke Ellington and as an heir to the speaking tradition of the great Afro-American preacher-orators, her personal style is expansive. Tall, buxom, and handsome, always elegantly dressed, she is charismatic, with a deep inner spirit. Her presence alone invites comparison to such warm performers as Ella Fitzgerald, B.B. King, and Duke Ellington, large in physical stature and large in spirit. As a public performer, her voice is deep and rich and thrilling, both as a speaker and singer. She is the type of person whose open-hearted energy is so overwhelmingly positive that her mere presence is inspiring to others. She literally radiates her inner love of humanity. In June 2001, her contributions to the community were recognized when she was awarded an honorary Doctor of Fine Arts degree by the University of Victoria.

Louise Rose gave individual lessons to Diana Krall in the early 1980s through the auspices of the community music school in Nanaimo. Louise recollects that these lessons took place every Saturday during the fall, winter, and spring in one of the piano studios at Malaspina University-College.

The Malahat Highway between Victoria and Nanaimo begins several miles north of the capital at Goldstream Provincial Park and winds its way over some of the most beautiful mountainous territory on the continent, but the highway is also one of the more hair-raising mountain drives in British Columbia, with its long roller-coaster-like hills and vertiginous bends with nothing but hard rock on one side and the empty space of cliffs on the other. Though smooth and well made, the Malahat requires every ounce of a driver's concentration even in good weather. In bad weather, the highway can be a total nightmare, especially in the winter when sudden rainstorms and snow are common on the upper reaches of the highway as well as impenetrably deep fogs. Saturday is the busiest day of the week on the highway, as Islanders travel back and forth from the capital city on business or on recreational tours, and it was always on Saturdays that Louise Rose made her trips to Nanaimo to meet with her young student there.

Louise Rose was likely the first full-fledged, full-time professional musician Diana had met in her life. This slightly shy, small-town girl must have felt more than a little intimidated and self-conscious meeting this worldly, former student of the same jazz giants who were her idols. "I vividly recall her first piano lesson," Louise notes, "because she was so nervous that she had small puddles of perspiration in each hand. I recall telling her that there was no reason for her to be nervous when we worked together because I wanted for her to have whatever she wanted to receive from the time we'd spend together. ... Diana was eager to learn. She was eager to play. And she listened well. She was also well supported (financially and emotionally) and encouraged by her family. ... I think the most important thing I ever told her was that she was capable and talented and that doing what she wanted to do would be hard work. The most important thing I showed her was how to sing and accompany herself in the honored style of those who'd preceded her." Louise taught Diana how to play "jazz standards with emphasis on piano style and piano voicings," and believes that she may have been the first to inform Diana that "playing and singing could be mutually inclusive." This information may have been "a catalyst for what she is doing now," Louise conjectures.

She also recalled passing on to Diana the 'lesson of all the lessons' she received from Oscar Peterson: the most difficult thing for artists is to learn to play like themselves. Louise suggests that Diana must have taken the lesson to heart because today she presents a style so fully and completely her own. "People compare her to Ella Fitzgerald," Louise notes. "They say Diana doesn't have the range. What a pity that we don't have the means to appreciate without making silly comparisons. But there is only one Ella, and there is only one Diana, too. Diana has the range that she has, and she *uses* it. She doesn't pretend to be anything other than she is. And you have to be confident about who you are in order to play like yourself."

Louise compared the criticism surrounding Diana's immense popularity to the criticism leveled at Miles Davis when he first became internationally famous, remarking that this was the product of "the jealousy of nay-sayers, a kind of self-loathing. If you're black you can't become too famous, or you will be accused of losing your soul," says Louise, implying that Diana has been a victim of similar criticism, but has not in the least lost any of her soul in consequence of her sudden celebrity. Concerning the criticism of her sultry image on her opulent album covers, Louis comments, "It goes to how they feel about the presentation of women. Come on! She's a sensuous, full-bodied *woman*, and she wants to show it!"

Louise Rose also cited the value of the West Coast jazz scene in the development of Diana's style. "I think it's something even more mystical than musical culture," she speculated. "There's something about a deeply spiritual culture that has supported folks like Diana Krall and Ross Taggart. I think something happens to people who live here. ... My personal experience is that people behave differently here, and when they tell you they *like* something, they like it at a *cellular* level. They seem to be saying the same words that other people say, but the way they behave toward the things they like is something else, something much deeper than the words alone can convey." She credits the people of Victoria and Nanaimo, often criticized for their social reserve, as some of the "warmest people I have met in my life, at a *soul* level" — and she clearly includes Diana Krall in this group. I can only begin to feel the effect this remarkable woman had upon the musical education and spiritual imagination of the young Diana Krall.

At the Berklee College of Music in Boston, Diana Krall must have encountered a very different world both in music and social life than she had seen before in her hometown. At the beginning, she felt a sense of conflict because she preferred the musical realm of her favorite jazz standards.

"I decided to take the chance and head to Berklee," Diana

says, "and though I had a far better grasp of the standards than my contemporaries there, I was criticized for playing old music. They said I wasn't playing fusion or funk, that I was behind the times. But I just stuck to my guns and played what I wanted to play."

During her months at Berklee, Diana recalls that she listened every night in her room to the work of arranger/composer Claus Ogerman, especially the album CITYSCAPE, Ogerman's collaboration with saxophonist Michael Brecker. The experience of listening to this music left an indelible impression on Diana. Even as a teenager she dreamed someday and somehow of working with Ogerman, a wish that was fulfilled in recording THE LOOK OF LOVE, where she plays those standards she studied at Berklee over Ogerman's string arrangements, played by the London Symphony Orchestra and the Los Angeles Session Orchestra. Recently, Diana has been recognized by her alma mater in a set of articles entitled, "For Diana Krall '83, the love of the music guides her course," appearing in *Berklee Today*, a magazine produced by Berklee students for the alumni.

At Berklee, Diana studied piano under Ray Santisi, an experienced pianist, who has played as a featured soloist with Charlie Parker, Stan Getz, Iren Kral, Natalie Cole, and other jazz greats. "Diana came into my office for her lesson once," Santisi recalls, "and I asked her to just sing a tune. I recognized immediately that she had a special quality to her voice. I said, 'Don't stop,' and she hasn't. Things have gone really well, and she has crossed over with her audience. You'd expect that she would attract kind of a conservative jazz crowd, but she has reached a much larger market. ...As a pianist, she was always into economy. She has said that she took a cue from comedians Alan King and Jack Benny whose punch lines were very economical. Diana has always been aware that you don't have to go grandstanding to make good music."

Santisi tells a story of meeting his now famous former student in Italy some years after she left Berklee. "A few years ago, I was doing a Berklee-in-Italy trip, and I met up with Tony Bennett there. Diana was playing in town at a little club called the Blue

Gardenia. Tony and I ended up getting front-row seats through Diana's manager Mary Ann Topper, who is a friend of mine. After the concert, we went backstage, and found Diana in tears. I told her what a beautiful set she had just played and asked her why she was crying. She said, 'I come out on stage, and sitting in the first row are Tony Bennett and my old piano teacher.'"

Diana did not complete her full two years of study at Berklee. By 1983 she was back in Nanaimo playing gigs in Victoria, Qualicum Beach, and other Vancouver Island towns, working with local professional musicians. She sometimes teamed up with Rick Kilburn, a bassist with considerable session experience who had played for two years with Dave Brubeck and another seven years with the quirky and marvelous pianist and singer from East Texas, Mose Allison. Kilburn recalls that Diana called him wanting to take lessons from him sometime around 1983 and 1984, but soon enough, they both discovered that Kilburn didn't have much to show Diana and began working together. Rick is the son of Vancouver jazz guitarist Jim Kilburn, who had played with Bryan Stovell and the others at the Cellar during the early '60s. Today he owns a small recording company in Burnaby, where he records up-and-coming young artists from the Pacific Northwest. He still plays professional gigs with the musicians in the Vancouver area, where his skills as a bass player are much admired, and in the past he has played with some very heavy jazz talent.

Diana would book gigs in the area, then call on Kilburn whenever she needed a bass player to back her up. Kilburn remembers playing hotel lounges and dinner gigs in Parksville, Victoria, and Nanaimo, as well as a show during the Alcan Jazz Competition in Vancouver at the Sheridan Landmark around 1984. They played standards from the classical American songbook, as Kilburn recalls. Diana and Rick became friends, and Kilburn sometimes visited the family home, where Diana was living at the time. Although Kilburn says she sang very little in those days, "You could always see where she was headed, and what she has done with it is fantastic, what can I say? She's had the good judgment to choose some great teachers and mentors. . . . She had a great ear, and she had an incredibly supportive upbringing. She was nurtured by her environment tremendously." Kilburn notes how her confidence as a performer has grown over the years. "One of the things that I like is the confidence she has gained since those days. People when they're young need to gain experience."

While she may have lacked confidence, Diana Krall certainly did not lack courage or determination. She persistently took measures to get around and make her music heard. In 1983, she attended the annual jazz festival held in the Washington Olympic Peninsula town of Port Townsend, across the Strait of Juan de Fuca from Victoria, where Bud Shank and other well-known West-Coast jazz musicians play and hold workshops for aspiring musicians. There, Diana met Jeff Hamilton, who had recently replaced the legendary Shelley Manne as drummer in the band known as the L.A. Four. The bass player in the L.A. Four was Ray Brown, a true jazz giant. The encounter with Jeff Hamilton turned out of the most fortunate in Diana's life thus far.

As it happened, Ray Brown was a frequent visitor to Nanaimo, where he went to visit friends and play the odd gig. Brown would usually play at Tio's, the restaurant which carried the name of the owner, a Vietnamese immigrant. The week following the festival in Port Townsend, Brown was in Nanaimo with the L.A. Four, and Hamilton pressed him to go to a local Nanaimo club to hear the young piano player he had just met. Brown was impressed. Brown and Hamilton were invited to the Krall family home for a dinner. There was both a dinner and a jam session at the Krall household that night, and much excited conversation. As journalist Dimetre Alexiou reports, "It was then that Hamilton told Adella Krall that her daughter could 'make it in jazz,' forcing her to alter her thinking. 'These musicians have distinguished careers,' Diana's mother recalls thinking. 'They're pretty real people.'" Brown suggested that Diana might have a great deal to gain by studying in Los Angeles, and that if Diana should decide this is what she wanted to do, she should call him there, and he would make the best arrangements possible.

If there is such a thing as royalty in the world of jazz, Ray

Brown, at 75 years old with more than 55 years as a professional musician under his belt, considered by many the greatest living jazz bassist, qualifies for one of its highest titles. In 1944, at the age of 19, Brown arrived in New York from his hometown of Pittsburgh. Already a polished performer on the double-bass, Brown was introduced in New York to the young Dizzy Gillespie. At that very moment in music history, Gillespie was gathering together the personnel to make up one of the most celebrated and influential small combos in the history of jazz, the Dizzy Gillespie Quintet. Hearing Brown play bass for the very first time, Gillespie hired Brown on the spot as a member of his new quintet. Brown joined a band featuring four of the greatest names in the history of jazz, each a remarkable musical revolutionary in his own right: trumpeter Dizzy Gillespie, alto-saxophonist Charlie Parker, pianist Bud Powell, and drummer Max Roach. This band led the Bebop revolution, which changed the sound of jazz during the final years of World War II.

The Dizzy Gillespie Quintet was only the beginning of Ray Brown's long and distinguished jazz career. In 1948, Brown formed his own trio and began recording and touring under his own name. During this same period, he also became involved with Norman Granz's Jazz at the Philharmonic, a large band with changing personnel that toured the world, winning fans for the new music everywhere. As organizer, impresario, and producer of Jazz at the Philharmonic, Granz became one of the most influential business figures in the history of North American music. Defying the color bar of racial segregation, Granz brought musicians from the older Swing tradition together with the new Bebop players — saxophonists Charlie Parker, Lester Young, Ben Webster, Flip Phillips, and Illinois Jacquet; pianists Bud Powell, Art Tatum, and Oscar Peterson; the Count Basie band; drummer Gene Krupa; trumpeters Dizzy Gillespie and Roy Eldridge; and, of course, the legendary Billie Holiday — all were at one time or another associated with Jazz at the Philharmonic ensembles. Ray Brown anchored many of these ensembles with his large, strong bass sound. Granz was later the founder of the well-known jazz oriented record label, Verve, which he sold to MGM Inc., in 1960. Still productive in the field of jazz, Verve produced Diana Krall's two most recent albums.

The Canadian-born pianist Oscar Peterson was Granz's chief lieutenant within the JATP ensemble. When Peterson set out on his own, Ray Brown became a member of the popular Oscar Peterson Trio for 18 years. During this time, he married the queen of jazz singers, Ella Fitzgerald, and even after their divorce continued to act as her manager. A giant in physical stature and musical prowess, and obviously in business acumen as well, Ray Brown has participated in more than 2000 recording sessions. There is probably no other musician on earth who can boast as many friends and acquaintances within the jazz world. A jazz statesman, Brown is revered by young jazz players and often promotes their careers. Diana Krall could never have found a better mentor and sponsor than jazz superstar Ray Brown.

With her reverence for the jazz tradition, Diana would have looked up to Ray Brown with nothing less than the most fervent respect. For his part, all reports indicate that Brown is very high on the talents of Diana as well. Jean-Michel Reisser, a European jazz impresario, concert organizer, sometime critic and a friend of Ray Brown comments, "Ray loves her very much and I can understand it because who possibly knows more about piano players and singers than Ray Brown? He played with every great pianist (Art Tatum, Oscar Peterson, Bud Powell, Hank Jones, Jimmie Rowles, Nat King Cole, Michel Petrucciani . . .) and every singer, too (Ella, of course, Sarah Vaughan, Dinah Washington, Billie Holiday, Carmen Marae, Peggy Lee, Linda Ronstadt, Joni Mitchell, Aretha Franklin, Dee Dee Bridgewater . . .)." In the liner notes Ray Brown wrote for Diana's first album in 1993, he remarks that listening to her music "is almost like listening to some of my own children playing." As Brown recalls, "I met Diana Krall in her hometown of Nanaimo in Canada. She was a teenage piano wiz. She called me some years ago to ask who she should study piano with and I recommended either Jimmy Rowles or Hank

Jones." Jones was busy at the time with another project, Brown continues the story, but "Jimmy Rowles was available and it has paid off handsomely."

———

Like Hank Jones, Jimmy Rowles belongs to a small group of elite mainstream jazz piano players whose names are little known to the general public, but who are regarded within the jazz world as the very best in their profession, both as piano soloists and accompanists. A sensitive player with a swinging style, Rowles began his career in the 1940s on the West Coast. After studying at the University of Washington and playing in bands around Seattle, he moved to Los Angeles, where he played with Lester Young's group in 1942, then with the local legend Slim Gaillard and Swing band leaders Benny Goodman and Woody Herman. He also had stints with Les Brown and Tommy Dorsey. For 25 years he composed and played music for Hollywood film soundtracks. After performing at the Newport Jazz Festival in 1973, he settled in New York, where he worked in clubs, mainly in duos with Zoot Sims, George Mraz, Buster Williams, and Stan Getz. The Los Angeles Jazz Society paid tribute to Rowles when he died on May 28, 1996. The distinguished jazz critic, Leonard Feather, wrote in commemoration: "Long acknowledged as the favorite of every singer, for whom he has played, Rowles was an artist of consummate harmonic imagination."

In Ken Burn's *Jazz* documentary, Rowles appears in several cameos. Singer Carol Sloane, a close friend of Rowles, remarks on his renowned humor and his "all-consuming humanity," describing his distinctive voice as "the sound of nails rattling in a tin can. Think Miles with laryngitis." She also recalls Rowles' convivial drinking habits. He would often engage in discussion with total strangers in his *"bar du jour*, regaling them with his curious and always hilarious drawings scrawled on cocktail napkins." But Jimmy Rowles is best known as an accompanist to some of the greatest female jazz singers of all time. He worked with Billie

Holiday and Peggy Lee in the 1940s and '50s, then he was the accompanist for Ella Fitzgerald in the 1980s.

Under the tutelage of Jimmy Rowles, the pianist with a voice "like nails in a can," Diana Krall began to inch toward the performance stage, not only as a young "piano wiz," but also, for the first time, as a singer with a voice like velvet. With obvious fondness, Diana recalls her days with Rowles in Los Angeles. "I consider myself fortunate to have had deep studies with Jimmy Rowles, which involved my knocking on his door whenever he felt good and was ready to see me. We'd hang out and listen to records all day, like Ben Webster and Duke Ellington." As Ray Brown describes the relationship between the elder jazzman and his new student, "He was so taken with her, he let her stay at the house with his daughter. He was like a father to her."

On the Bravo Arts & Minds video *Diana Krall in Nanaimo*, she recounts some special experiences with Rowles. "You know, Jimmy Rowles would sit there talking about 'Beauty, Diana.' He'd put on DAPHNIS AND CHLOE. Jimmy Rowles used to sit there and say, 'You're trying to play so fast. Here, play this. (She makes a gesture indicating a quick movement to put a record into her hand). You forget about the beauty of what you're doing.' I was a 19-year-old kid. I was *trying* to play fast. Then, I got it," Diana says, a sense of relief and gratitude showing in her posture.

If she had remained a pianist and never become a singer, Diana Krall might still be struggling to achieve her professional reputation even today, but as the singer-pianist that she became under the guidance of Jimmy Rowles, Diana entered the jazz world with a full repertoire of musical accomplishments. After her bold decision to move to Los Angeles to study jazz piano, the decision to become a singer was probably the most important in Diana's young career. The decision to become a singer in Los Angeles may have been assisted by necessity, as Ray Brown recalls. "I went down to this little club to hear her. She was kinda sad. I said 'What's wrong?' She said, 'They're going to revoke my card.' And for some reason . . . I don't know what this law was, but they said if she sang, she could stay, but if she didn't sing, she had to go back to Canada. So I said, 'Hell with it, sing. Go ahead and sing!'"

In the Bravo TV production *An Evening with Diana Krall*, produced some time after the success of LOVE SCENES, Diana reflects upon her decision to become a singer. "I always sang privately, because I was very shy. Singing is much more personal. . . . I sang because I learned the lyrics. I felt it was important to learn the words, to learn everything about the tune . . . to respect the song. I started messing around with singing in high school, but it wasn't until I moved to LA that it got serious. I'd go to auditions, and they'd ask, 'Do you sing?' And I'd say: 'Okay.' . . . I was just playing piano then. I had no confidence in my voice at all — it was kind of low, had a smoky sound, and I thought it lacked expressiveness." She would sometimes sing if club managers asked her, but in her own words, "only enough to keep the gig."

One of the side benefits of becoming the protégée of Ray Brown and Jimmy Rowles was the acquaintances Diana made with their circle of friends. Within their circle are found the finest musicians from the oldest New Orleans players to the youngest and brightest new talents on the scene. Two of these young musicians were John Clayton and Jeff Hamilton, both of whom became members of Ray Brown's own trio and later played with Diana. John Clayton became associated with Brown at the age of 16, in the same way that Diana had — as his student. Today, he still calls Brown "Pops." At the age of 19, he was the bassist on Henry Mancini's television series *The Mancini Generation*, after which he went to Indiana University to complete his studies and then graduated to a position as bassist in the Count Basie Orchestra. In 1984, just as Diana was moving to Los Angeles, Clayton was settling into the city after returning to the United States from serving five years as principal bassist of the Amsterdam Philharmonic Orchestra. Within a year, Clayton and his brother, saxophonist Jeff Clayton, had teamed up with the drummer Jeff Hamilton to form the Clayton-Hamilton Jazz Orchestra. Of Clayton's arranging and composing work, Leonard Feather has remarked he is "one of the six best possibilities to assume the mantle of Miles Davis."

Live in Singapore, 2001

Massey Hall, Toronto, 1998

Hollywood Bowl, 2001

Toronto, 2000

Toronto, 2000

Indigo Books, Music & Café, 1999

Diana Krall and Sarah McLachlan, Grammy Awards, 2000

Best Jazz Vocal Performance, Grammy Awards, 2000

John Clayton is "rapidly becoming one of the most internationally respected bassists and composers, with good reason." Performer, arranger, composer, teacher, mentor, and all around brilliant musician, both in the jazz and the classical field, he has served as president of the 1500-member International Bassist Association. In 1998, he became the Artistic Director of Jazz for the Los Angeles Philharmonic and the Hollywood Bowl.

Jeff Hamilton, the drummer in the Clayton-Hamilton Jazz Orchestra, also served his apprenticeship as a member of the Oscar Peterson trio. Writing about Hamilton's work with the Peterson group, Leonard Feather notes that his "intelligent backing and spirited solo work met Peterson's customarily high standards." Oscar Peterson is known in the jazz world as a perfectionist. Once asked, "When do you stop working on a tune?" he replied, "When it's perfect. Not before." Hamilton's professional career began with a stint in 1974 with the Tommy Dorsey Orchestra. He then joined Lionel Hampton's band in 1975, and in 1977 began to work with Woody Hermans Thundering Herd. In 1978, he took over the position occupied by Shelley Manne in the group known as the L.A.4, featuring Ray Brown, the popular reed player Bud Shank, and the guitarist Laurindo Almeida. Brown himself describes Jeff Hamilton as "possibly the most versatile drummer since Shelley Manne." High praise, indeed. He, too, would become a player in Diana Krall's trio.

Diana Krall remained in Los Angeles, studying and playing, and sometimes singing, for the better part of three years. Sometime in 1987 or 1988, she returned to Canada and decided to move to Toronto. In Canada, an artistic or music career can only be assisted by moving closer to the centers of cultural power. Those centers are Toronto for English-speaking Canada and Montreal for French-speaking Canada, just as the cultural centers in the United States are in New York and Los Angeles. In Canada, it's almost compulsory to move to Toronto or Montreal if you want to enjoy a national career with a national following, just as American musicians and entertainers must move to New York and Los Angeles.

Diana had already been introduced to many of the jazz artists in Toronto when she traveled to the city with Bryan Stovell in the early 1980s. There she first met the trombonist John Capon, Stovell's former University of British Columbia friend, and still a sometime resident of British Columbia who owns a home on Galiano Island off the coast from Nanaimo. She had also already met Don Thompson, a brilliant multi-instrumentalist, composer, bandleader, bandsman, and arranger, originally from Vancouver.

Don Thompson's career has interesting parallels to Diana's. He was born in the pulp-mill town of Powell River, a town that can only be reached by water, either on a ferry from Vancouver Island or from the northern tip of the southern British Columbia coastal region known as the Sunshine Coast. Thompson attended the University of British Columbia with John Capon, Bryan Stovell, Jerry Fuller, and Stanley Clarke. During his early professional career in Vancouver, he played in groups led by Dave Robbins, Chris Gage, and Fraser McPherson, and appeared on CBC radio and television as a featured artist and bandleader. After a few years apprenticeship in Canada, he linked up with an American jazz musician and traveled in the United States, later returning to Canada and Toronto to establish the respected place in Canada's music scene he now occupies today.

This is a familiar career pattern for Canadian-born jazz musicians. Canadian musicians are drawn to America, where some of the greatest jazz players live, where they can hear the best musicians and the widest variety of styles, where the young jazz player can most easily learn the profession and find work. The best jazz players are those who open up their horizons, play with musicians of every stripe, mastering different styles in the crucible of live performance.

Don Thompson, a young musician in the 1960s, like Diana later, found a way to travel to the United States and practice his music there. His chance came in 1965 when the lyrical and passionate saxophonist John Handy, a recent graduate of the Charles

Mingus band, came to Vancouver to give a performance in the ballroom at the Vancouver Hotel. As was often the case, touring solo musicians were backed up by a local rhythm section. Don Thompson was in the rhythm section backing up John Handy, who was impressed enough with his playing to hire him as a member of his quintet. Handy's quintet recorded two albums with Columbia. One of these recordings, JOHN HANDY LIVE AT THE MONTEREY JAZZ FESTIVAL, achieved a kind of legendary status and became one of the most popular jazz albums of the 1960s. During a stay in San Francisco, Thompson also worked with the trumpeter Frank Rosolino, Canadian-born Maynard Ferguson, keyboardist George Duke, and Danny Zeitlin.

Two years later in 1967, Thompson returned to Canada and joined Rob McConnell's Boss Brass as a percussionist, switching to bass in 1971 and later to piano (1987-1983). He worked with Moe Koffman from 1970 to 1979 alternately as pianist and bassist, contributing arrangements and compositions as the co-producer of two Koffman albums, MUSEUM PIECES and LOOKING UP. He also worked extensively with the Canadian guitarists Ed Bickert, Lenny Breau, and Sonny Greenwich. For years, he worked as a member of the "house rhythm section" at Toronto's Bourbon Street Jazz Club, where he was heard backing up jazz celebrities like Paul Desmond, Jim Hall, Milt Jackson, Art Farmer, James Moody, Zoot Sims, Clark Terry, Harry Edison, Frank Rosolino, Slide Hampton, Lee Konitz, and Abbey Lincoln. Outside the context of Bourbon Street, he also worked with Sarah Vaughan, Red Rodney, Joe Henderson, Dewey Redman, Red Mitchell, Sheila Jordan, and Kenny Wheeler. He toured in Europe and Japan, as well as the United States and Canada, with Jim Hall's trio in 1974. In 1982 he joined the great British jazz pianist George Shearing on a tour that took him to almost every major jazz club and festival in the United States, then on to Great Britain and Brazil.

A multi-talented instrumentalist, Thompson is an expressive musician able to make music on vibes, piano, bass, and drums. His teaching credentials are equally impressive, and he is also a fully competent and trusted sound engineer who runs a studio out of his home in Toronto. Diana Krall could not have chosen a better mentor in Toronto. Don Thompson, a fellow British Columbian from a maritime B.C. town with a pulp-mill past, the old friend of her home-town music teacher, Bryan Stovell, was the very best that Canada had to offer. Working as often as she was able to find gigs, Diana also continued to develop her musicianship while studying under Don Thompson. "He really encouraged me to not have an analytical approach," she comments. "He taught me to listen and transcribe and really use my ear. He knows all the theory, but he told me to learn all that, then play what I feel. He said it's really important to play what's inside you."

While Diana may have been assisted in her move to Toronto by a grant from the Canada Council for the Arts and encouraged by previous mentors, her economic condition was uncertain after her arrival as she tried to break into the new scene. No matter what past credentials she brought with her from Los Angeles, no matter her contacts with local musicians, she had to win respect and trust. Concerning those early Toronto months, she comments, "Everybody goes through that . . . You're new on the scene. You're a woman. And you're not sure what you can do. People get over the initial, 'Wow, here's this woman piano player.' When you're young, you're more concerned with that because nobody knows you." Diana has never made much of the fact that she is a *woman* in jazz, a world dominated by men, where women are often stereotyped as only singers, "canaries." There is even a joke in the jazz world that goes like this: Question: "What do singers and drummers have in common?" Answer: "They both like to hang around with musicians."

During this same period, Diana and her family suffered a serious loss with the death in 1988 of her grandmother, the same grandmother who in Diana's childhood had organized the weekly family dinners where the Krall family sang and played music together with their friends. In an interview 12 years after her grandmother's death, Diana reflected, sadly, that "she never got to see any of this. Unfortunately, she died when I was 24, which really sucks. Every day I think about it. She would have been so happy. I was very close to her."

Diana's circumstances in Toronto were made somewhat easier by the fact that she was invited to stay at the home of Enid MacLachlan, the mother-in-law of John Capon, a professional trombonist, a British Columbia native, and another friend of Bryan Stovell. According to Stovell, Diana stayed there for the full two years of her sojourn in Toronto. Ms. McLachlan told me that "the kids" (John Capon and his wife, Tawny) informed her that Diana was moving to Toronto to study with Don Thompson and asked her, "'Mom, how would you like to look after her.' I said, 'sure.'" With a modest maternal pride, she credits her son for recognizing Diana's vocal abilities, telling his mother that "besides her jazz piano, it's going to be her voice that makes her famous."

Enid McLachlan came to Canada as a "British war bride," having married a Canadian seaman, Peter MacLachlan, and traveled to North America on the *Queen Elizabeth*, landing at New York and finally settling in Toronto in 1947. A graduate from a London arts school, she became an arts administrator, serving as a trustee of the prestigious Art Gallery of Ontario, and later acting as chair of the Arts Commission in Toronto. At the time Diana came to Toronto, Diana was 24 years old and Ms. McLachlan was approaching normal retirement age.

Twelve years later, the affection Enid MacLachlan still holds for Diana Krall underscores the kind of loyalty she seems to inspire in everyone with whom she works and lives. "I love Diana," Ms. McLachlan volunteers. "The one thing that Diana is wonderful about is she takes care of her friends. She still calls me on my birthday. Sometimes she used to call me late at night from wherever she was in Europe or the States. She doesn't do it much these days, because she's so busy." Ms. McLachlan allows that Diana did come to dinner at her home during her last visit to Toronto "just before Christmas. And I much appreciated it."

"When she was living here, she really knew how to work hard . . . She was earning her living here as a musician," Ms McLachlan says, "and she had to work hard at finding gigs. . . . She put together a Curriculum Vitae while she was here. The photographer

John Reeves took photographs, and she used them to put together her portfolio."

For a while, there was no piano in the house for Diana to use, but a piano was finally rented and moved into Ms. McLachlan's home. In the interim, Diana sometimes went to the home of a friend to use the piano there, and sometimes, too, Enid McLachlan believes, she went to the Toronto Conservatory of Music to practice. I told Ms. McLachlan that I had read somewhere that Diana used to practice piano after hours at the Café des Copains on Wellington Street. "Anywhere she could find a piano, she would take the opportunity to practice."

Ms. McLachlan says she often used to go to Diana's gigs, "to take care of her." When I suggested, "As a chaperone?" she responded, "Well, not going that far, of course. What used to bother me was the people who wouldn't listen to her music, talking too loudly while she was playing and banging cutlery, that used to make me angry." She remembers several charity performances that Diana played, and one gig where she played at an opening for her son-in-law at Gallery One in Toronto. Diana once traveled to the Canadian Maritimes for a short stint in a hotel there. She also remembers that Sybil Martin, who was responsible for booking acts at the Top of the Senator in Toronto, shared her affection for Diana and tried to do Diana favors in terms of providing gigs for her. Ms. McLachlan's main concern about Diana today is that she has to work too hard. She once asked Diana, after she had begun to tour with her own band, "When do you sleep?" "I put my head on Russell [Malone]'s shoulder on the plane," Diana replied.

In Toronto, Diana certainly paid her dues. Bill King, artistic director of the Beaches Jazz Festival in Toronto and publisher of the international quarterly magazine, *The Jazz Report*, first saw Diana perform with a small combo at Meyer's Deli in Toronto's Yorkville area. As he recollected while interviewing Diana some years later concerning her Toronto years, "Like so many Canadian musicians, you suffered through weekend gigs like Meyer's Deli in Yorkville," King commented, "where orders for corned beef sandwiches and *Hockey Night In Canada* drowned out the music at the other end of the room. Soon you were able to move downtown to the Underground Railroad [a restaurant serving mainly 'soul food'], where you attracted a listening audience." Diana picked up the thread of this story. "The Underground Railroad was about two people," she recalled, "John Henry and his wife. They believed in what I wanted to do and gave me an opportunity. I was talking with John Clayton about this at the International Association of Jazz Educators' conference. We were discussing the importance of recognizing an individual's ability and giving them a good environment in which to grow. I also believe you should want to make people happy with what you are doing. Rather than bypass certain gigs, I created the kind of work that would help me grow as an artist even though at times I was compelled to eat in a cafeteria and not fraternize with the guests. I was directed to go downstairs and drink my cup of coffee with the hired help. That wasn't respectful to me as an artist, but I've always decided to make each place my own and hire the best musicians possible."

There are also stories from this same period of Diana remaining behind after the set at the Café des Copains, a club on Wellington Street which often featured touring piano stylists. There she would play at the piano for hours, simply practicing her art for whatever crowd remained after the feature performers had stopped playing, taking every opportunity to practice live on stage. The remaining crowd, according to Sybil Walker, mainly the cleaning staff at that hour, was willing to listen until the earliest hours of the morning.

"Thank you Ross Porter; Katie Malloch; Neil Ritchie; Jurgen Gothe; Peter Gzowski; and everyone at CBC," Diana Krall writes on the liner of album ALL FOR YOU. Without the recognition she received these individuals working with the Canadian Broadcasting Company, Diana Krall's music may not have reached the public ear. There is no commercial station in Vancouver or elsewhere in Canada that consistently supports jazz artists, but the publicly owned CBC often programs jazz, broadcasting live concerts or studio sessions, and promotes new talent coast-to-coast-to-coast. Besides broadcasting the music of young artists, the CBC provides recording studios that are technically capable of producing finer records than these artists might otherwise be able to afford on their own. The CBC tapes can be used as demos in the effort to win first recording contracts. Apart from recording and broadcasting their music, CBC pays probably the best rates available and royalties on every subsequent playing of the tapes.

From the very beginning of her career when she was known to no one except a small coterie of fans in Nanaimo and Vancouver, the CBC has been making Diana Krall's music available to the Canadian public. Even today, it is hard to imagine another broadcaster that would have produced the television special *Diana Krall in Paris* broadcast on January 13, 2001. Diana made her first tapes with CBC Vancouver in 1992, and another set were made for broadcast in 1993, produced by Neil Ritchie, a fan of jazz vocal music who has been the head of a show broadcast from CBC Radio in Vancouver called *Hot Air* for the past 22 years. Although Ritchie had reservations about Diana's potential to become a major jazz force, feeling she lacked the charisma to communicate with a large audience, he sent the tapes on to the *Jazz Beat* program on Montreal's CBC, then across the network. Because of these CBC broadcasts, people first began not only to hear her music but also to talk about Diana Krall as an-up-and-coming jazz artist, including hosts of national programs like Ross Porter, Katie Malloch, Jurgen Gothe, and Peter Gzowski. Today, Neil Ritchie has no reservations about Diana Krall's charisma.

Another Canadian institution that has supported Diana over the years is the Canada Council of the Arts. Between 1984 and 1994, she received no fewer than six Canada Council grants. She received her first award in 1984 to help her finance the move to Los Angeles to study with Jimmy Rowles. According to a Canada Council librarian, Diana also received grants in 1985, 1987, 1990, 1991, and 1994. Confidentiality regulations prevent the employees of the Council from revealing the amount of grants given to individual artists, but the Council librarian told me that the grants given to Diana were of two main types, annual subsistence grants and project grants. While Diana received one such subsistence grant for a maximum of $20,000, she was assisted with several projects to pursue mentorship programs. These Canada Council grants not only helped ends meet but enabled her to work with her mentors. Diana has remarked that even as late as 1996, before ALL FOR YOU began to achieve bestseller status, she was still having trouble making the rent each month.

──────────

From one perspective, Diana Krall's career may seem to have been carefully plotted — first we take Los Angeles, then we take Toronto, then Manhattan. But it is far more likely that the young pianist was just following her nose when she left Toronto for New York in 1990.

There is no jazz artist anywhere who does not dream of playing music in the birthplace of modern jazz. A mere glance at the entertainment pages of the *New York Times* or the *New Yorker* magazine is enough to verify the fact that New York, on any given night of the year, offers more jazz than any other city on the continent or in the world. There are more than twenty jazz venues in Manhattan, with a similar number in Queens and Brooklyn, including Birdland, the Blue Note, the Village Vanguard, the Knitting Factory, the Oak Room at the Algonquin Hotel, Arturo's, the Lenox Lounge, the Metronome Jazz Lounge, the Knickerbocker Saloon, not to speak of the legendary theaters and night clubs, the Copacabana, Carnegie Hall, the Cotton Club, the Lincoln Center, and the Apollo Theatre. In the next ten months, at least 75 internationally-recognized bands are scheduled to play in New York, including Paul Motian and the Electric Bebop Band, the Mike Rossi Quintet, the Hank Jones Trio, Ron Carter, Flora Purim and Airto, John Scofield, Roy Hargrove, Toshiko Ashiyoka Jazz Orchestra, McCoy Tyner, David Sanborn, Herbie Hancock, Billy Cobham, Ahmad Jamal, Sam Rivers, Pharoah Sanders, and Jackie McLean and the Mingus Big Band. There are numerous jazz tributes, too — for Joe

Henderson and Miles Davis. The Wynton Marsalis Orchestra was recently joined by Pharoah Sanders in a tribute to John Coltrane. Diana Krall herself is listed for two performances at the end of March 2002 at Radio City Hall.

New York is also the headquarters of some the world's largest recording companies, and literally dozens, perhaps hundreds of smaller record labels. Every jazz musician who wants to 'break out' of local or regional circumstances will inevitably head for New York. Diana Krall was 26 years old when she moved to New York, with 11 years of musical apprenticeship behind her, still without a commercial recording to her own name, still untested on the North American club circuit outside of Los Angeles or Toronto. While she may have had designs on a recording contract, Diana was primarily motivated to move to New York by a pure musical desire. She went to New York to listen and to learn. "I knew I had to go to New York at some point," she observes, "because that's the center. I wanted to go and hear Cedar Walton, Tommy Flanagan, Clark Terry and Ray Brown. I've met so many people in my life just through liking them, admiring their work. ... I mean, I've met them and had a chance to learn from them."

Some time after her arrival in the city, Diana met with the musicians who made up a new trio, the drummer Klaus Suonsaari and the bassist Whit Browne. Together with this trio she began a weekly series of gigs at the Boston Harbor Hotel in Boston, commuting every weekend from New York to play a seven-hour set, and then returning to live in New York throughout the week.

The dignified arches on the façade of the Boston Harbor Hotel say nothing about any music that might be heard within, but the hotel managers insisted that the woman who played piano in the trio that they hired must also sing as part of her contract. The shy chanteuse was forced to bite the bullet and sing on every blessed night of her engagement at the Boston Harbor Hotel. Today she credits the four years spent singing weekends in the bar at the hotel with giving her the opportunity to learn how to vocalize. "It was when I realized that I had the creative freedom to be the artist I really wanted to be," Diana notes, "without worrying about compromising what I had to do. I worked really hard commuting to a gig in Boston while living in New York for about four years. Even with a recording out, I was still doing it. . . . As a new artist, I was struggling to make a living, but it was an opportunity to keep learning and playing especially since it was a seven-hour gig per night. It was hard schlepping through the snow and the long train rides, but I wanted to stay in New York."

Diana's Boston Harbor Hotel engagement had been booked for her by Mary Ann Topper's The Jazz Tree, a well-respected management company for jazz artists. Neil Ritchie of CBC Vancouver's *Hot Air* jazz program credits Mary Ann Topper with impressing upon Diana important lessons in stage presence, above all the importance of creating an appealing and glamorous stage image. Mary Ann Topper also introduced Diana to guitarist Russell Malone, bassist Paul Keller, and pianist Benny Green, who would eventually appear on her albums. In the liner notes to LOVE SCENES, Diana's thankyou section contains an effusive tribute to Mary Ann Topper: "To Mary Ann, we've come a long way from that snowy day in February. You have given me such insight into so many things, and I appreciate it so very much. Your never-ending passion for your artists and this music is inspiring. We'll look forward to that safari! Lots of love to you, and thank you." Diana adds another thank you to "my management team at Jazz Tree: Mary Ann, Anna, Rick, Maya, Matt, and Julia — You are the greatest support system ever."

By 1992, two years after leaving Toronto for New York, Diana at last felt ready to undertake the next project in her career, the making of her first record. Recorded in Los Angeles with her old friends John Clayton and Jeff Hamilton, STEPPING OUT was released by Justin Time Records of Montreal in 1993. Label manager Jim West arranged for her debut at the Blue Note, a smashing performance that caught the eye of executives from GRP Records. A year later, her second album, ONLY TRUST YOUR HEART, was recorded in New York City by GRP Records, from September 13–16. Since then, Diana Krall has been a resident of New York and a fixture in the New York jazz scene.

Stepping Out with
Diana **K**rall

When Diana Krall released her first album in 1993, she was already 29 years old. She had been playing jazz piano professionally for 15 years and accompanying her own singing in public for a least 10 years. Pressed by an interviewer to explain why her first recording appeared so late in her career, Diana would only say, "I wasn't ready."

The album would probably never have seen the light of day, if not for the support Diana received from her friends from her Los Angeles days, especially Ray Brown. Diana prepared a demo tape in which she was joined by Brown's protégés, bassist John Clayton and the drummer Jeff Hamilton. The demo succeeded in winning a record deal with the Justin Time label in Montreal, Quebec. The website for the label heralds Justin Time as Canada's largest independent jazz recording company. The label proudly announces the first Grammy nominations it has ever received: "The nominations for the upcoming Grammy Awards have been announced and Justin Time has seen two of its artists and recordings nominated for awards. Russell Gunn and his album ETHNOMUSICOLOGY — VOLUME 2 were nominated in the Best Contemporary Jazz Album category. The Rob McConnell Tentet and their eponymous album were nominated in the Best Large Jazz Ensemble

Album category. These are the first Grammy nominations Justin Time Records has received for recordings it has produced."

"Montrealer Jim West founded Justin Time Records in 1983," the notice continues. "The label's first recording, inspired by a particularly swinging evening at a local jazz club, was also pianist Oliver Jones' first foray into jazz as a leader. Since then, the label has released more than 300 recordings. Although Justin Time is recognized mainly as a jazz label, its catalogue of recordings also features albums in the musical genres of blues, gospel, world, comedy, film soundtracks and folk." Among the label's 300 recordings are the names of many internationally known Canadian jazz artists: Paul Bley, Jane Bunnett, Kenny Colman, Wray Downes, Maynard Ferguson, Sonny Greenwich, Ingrid Jensen, Oliver Jones, Moe Koffman, Fraser MacPherson, the Rob McConnell Tentet, P.J. Perry, Oscar Peterson, Herbie Spanier, and Kenny Wheeler. The label has also recorded well-known American and international stars like Chet Baker, James Cotton, Reverend Gary Davis, Dizzy Gillespie, Stephane Grapelli, John Lee Hooker, Lightnin' Hopkins, the Pat LaBarbera Quartet, Archie Shepp, Sonny Terry and Brownie McGhee, the Ed Thigpen Trio, Big Mama Thornton, Sarah Vaughan, Joe Venuti & Tony Romano, and Muddy Waters.

Jim West recalls the history of recording Diana's first album. "Diana sent her tape to us," he explains, "but she was also mentioned to us by Oliver Jones' former manager Carol Clark. In addition, there were calls from CBC producers and quite possibly Jacques Emond from the Ottawa Jazz Fest. Oliver talked to me about Diana as well, encouraging us to do something with her, and Denis Barnabé from our office went to Boston to see her perform in a hotel, and was impressed. I then met with Diana and Carol Clark in Kingston, Ontario to discuss doing a record. So we sent her a contract, and that's the way it all started. We then asked Diana to open for the Montreal Jubilation Gospel Choir at their Christmas Concert, which she did."

As West continues his account, "her first main manager was Mary Ann Topper. We collectively set up and paid for a showcase at the Blue Note in NYC and invited all the major labels and media to attend. It was a huge success. This is where GRP (now Universal) saw her and came to us to basically buy out her contract. We originally wanted to license all productions to them but they wanted to take over the whole deal. The rest is history.

"The record has been widely available since its release in 1993, and we in fact licensed this in Europe to Enja Records, but there was a period of time when GRP licensed it from us and released it in the U.S.A. as STEPPING OUT: THE EARLY RECORDINGS. When this deal ended, we added one new song and remastered it, releasing it as a proper Justin Time recording for the first time in the U.S.A. (Universal had wanted to keep the rights but obviously we wanted back the rights)."

Diana's album from Justin Time is aptly and wittily named STEPPING OUT, reflecting several meanings — the obvious slang meaning of making a public display, the allusion to the first dance of the nervous debutante, and the honest confession of a jazz musician daring to take her first step into the world of recorded jazz. The album cover features a very simple photograph of an attractive, blond young woman, simply dressed in a beige suit jacket and a black blouse. Although her appearance is fresh, almost dewy, no one would call the presentation glamorous. She looks pensive, reflective, almost introverted. Diana's demeanor is more like a graduate student at university than a worldly-wise jazz musician. She looks outward and away from the camera as if lost in thought, in a moment of private reverie.

Inside the album, Diana appears slightly tough-looking in a photo where her artfully-tousled coppery blond hair emerges in three dimensions from the flatly rendered black of her turtle neck sweater. The solitary figure is surrounded by a lushly lit, but empty background, darkening from a peachy beige light at the bottom to a rich red brown at the top. The singer gazes straight out of the frame, as if to lock eyes with the viewer. Her jaw is set and there is a slight droop to the right upper eyelid, lending her an appearance appealingly sceptical and resolute, a look at once determined and self-respecting while also seeming to seek respect and acceptance in return. A smaller photo on the back of the album shows Diana with hands locked in front of her knees, gazing outward in such a way as to appear to fix her gaze resolutely on the viewer — a look slightly challenging and at the same time slightly defensive, as if to say, "Yes, this is me. I am a woman jazz singer and piano player. This is the real goods, whether you like it or not."

The record is, in fact, the real goods, a smashing jazz debut. There are 11 tracks, ranging from romantic standard ballads such as *This Can't Be Love, Body And Soul,* and *Between The Devil And The Deep Blue Sea,* to humorous novelty standards like *Straighten Up And Fly Right* and *Do Nothin' Till You Hear From Me.* Most of the tunes are oft-played standards, even chestnuts, part of the beginning repertoire of any aspiring jazz musician. Besides the eight vocal tracks, there are three purely instrumental tracks. *Jimmie,* as noted by Ray Brown in his liner note, is a tribute to Diana's father, Jim Krall, and her former teacher and mentor, pianist Jimmy Rowles. The tune is composed by Diana herself (the only instance of the appearance of her own composition on any of her albums so far). *42nd Street,* by Dubin and Warren, is obviously included in the album as a tribute to the jazz musicians who played on that famous New York avenue of jazz. *Big Foot,* the third instrumental, was composed by Diana's former band-member, Klaus Suonsaari. The light-hearted, uplifting chestnut, *On the Sunny Side of the Street,* was included on a re-release of the record in 2000. Listening to the album, it's easy to feel that John Clayton and Jeff Hamilton were bent on putting all their talent behind this showcase of Diana's playing and singing. Surrounded by the best of personnel and taking on some favorite tunes, Diana Krall steps out in style.

Most records contain 10 or 12 tracks, but of those, two or three, or at most four or five, are given the full treatment. They are the real meat of the record. Often, the rest of rest of the album is filler, even second-rate material. There are very few recording artists who give their full attention to every tune on the album, and this is even more often true in first recordings. There is no second-rate material on STEPPING OUT, in the same way as there is no filler on any of the other albums Diana has ever made. Listeners will appreciate that every tune fits into its own place within the concept of the album. Each song arrives in as polished and as complete a form as the three musicians on the album are able to deliver. Diana maintains this same exacting standard of professional perfectionism in every album from her first to her most recent.

STEPPING OUT begins with a spirited and humorous rendition of the Rodgers and Hart classic, *This Can't Be Love*. Diana's voice is suitably raunchy and funky, clipped and sardonic.

This can't be love because I feel so well
No sobs, no sorrows, no sighs
This can't be love I get no dizzy spells
My head is not in the skies . . .
— RODGERS/HART

Diana's vocal presentation is deliberately slightly tough, sometimes nasal, as she seems to be attempting to achieve a mature, world-weary tonality that is nonetheless playful. Although this feature seems to be an attempt to imitate previous blues artists in vocal tonality, the overall feel of the tune remains that of a distinctive performer who already sounds like no one else but herself.

The piano-playing is brisk and smart, impelled by a smooth walking bass from John Clayton, punctuated with sharp stabs from Diana's left hand, a tumultuous rollicking solo, complemented with snappy brush work by drummer Jeff Hamilton.

The second song, the novelty tune *Straighten Up And Fly Right*, is in the same humorous vein. Diana's hard-driving piano recalls the left-hand comping of Errol Garner. The song features a convincingly subtle and melodic brush solo by Hamilton, just before Diana's piano coda.

Between The Devil And The Deep Blue Sea has no vocal. It is a bravura performance by Diana on the piano, accompanied by Jeff Hamilton's slick and swish drum stylings. A medium tempo, swinging romp. Not too fast, not too slow. Just right.

I'm Just A Lucky So And So begins with a slow and bluesy solo by Diana, once again slightly nasal, slightly tough, but with subtle changes of tempo and intonation, Diana brings off a convincingly traditionalist blues performance here, full of happiness and elan.

When I walk down the street
Seems everyone I meet
Gives me a friendly hello
I guess I'm just a lucky so and so

The birds in every tree
All sing so merrily
They sing wherever I go
I guess I'm just a lucky so and so

. . . And when my day is through
Each night I hurry to
A love that's faithful I know
I guess I'm just a lucky so and so

    – ELLINGTON/DAVID

Body And Soul is a true classic jazz classic standard. The song has been performed by many different vocal artists, including Billie Holiday and Sarah Vaughan, and by instrumentalists as well — most notably Coleman Hawkins, whose treatment of the song is universally acknowledged as a breakthrough jazz masterpiece. Even to dare to choose this tune is an act of courage, given its hallowed history.

My heart is sad and lonely
For you I sigh, for you dear only
Why haven't you seen it?
I'm all for you body and soul . . .

Looks like the ending
Unless I could have one more chance to prove

Dear, my life's a wreck you're making
You know that I'm yours for just the taking
I'd gladly surrender body and soul
– GREEN/HEYMAN/SOUR/EYTON

Diana's piano is quiet and impressionistic, drawing its effects from splashes of notes and chords surrounded by slow comping in the bass register. Her vocal is also appropriately quiet. As Ray Brown says in the liner notes, "there is a lot of soul inside this lady." The piano playing is without doubt soulful, establishing the mood from which the vocal comes, though some of Diana's vocal embellishments seem just that, embellishments rather than direct access to the emotion.

The next song, the straightforward instrumental *42nd Street*, seems obviously intended as an evocation of Diana's attitude to her roots in modern jazz — 42nd Street being the home of the jazz clubs in New York that sponsored the Bebop revolution in the 1940s and later became the staging ground of all the diverse trends that continued to bubble up in new music. The mood of the tune owes a great deal to the interplay between Jeff Hamilton's always-melodic drumming and Diana's rhythmic piano.

Another jazz chestnut, *Do Nothin' Till You Hear From Me* is the seventh song on the album. Diana's vocals are lighter and fresher on this piece. Her presentation evokes an independent-minded young woman speaking to a possibly jealous lover who has heard rumors that she has been seen with "someone new." Instead of a conciliatory tone, Diana adopts a humorously challenging tone, at the same time frank and confident, reassuring the doubtful lover with bracing admonitions not to believe anyone else until he hears directly from the lover herself. John Clayton plays a lovely and unexpected arco solo in the middle of the tune, with strong echoes of the violin of Stephane Grapelli, the unparalleled band mate of Django Reinhardt.

Big Foot is another instrumental, done in traditional trio style. The rhythm section of Clayton and Hamilton cooks steadily behind a stream of inventive, bluesy improvisations by Diana on piano. The middle of the tune features a friendly, conversational arco solo by Clayton, punctuated lightly by Diana's accompaniment. Brown's liner notes speak of the exchange of "fours" between Diana and Jeff Hamilton. Brown remarks on his own pride as a former teacher and mentor to Hamilton, noting that the drummer actually "plays solos that sound like music and not drum rudiments," obviously a rare and valuable quality in a drummer.

Another tune from the song book of Nat King Cole, *Frim Fram Sauce* becomes again a vehicle for Diana's suggestive humor. Her vocal delivery is slyly conversational, strongly implying that something else besides Cajun food ("frim-fram sauce and sha fa fa on the side") is the subject of the song. Another rollicking piano solo from Diana is complemented by yet another supreme drum solo from Jeff Hamilton.

Diana's own composition, *Jimmie*, a tribute to the two men called Jimmy in her life, her father, and her recent mentor, Jimmy Rowles, opens with a moody and lyrical arco solo by Clayton, which is followed by an equally lyrical and reflective solo by Diana, evoking the mood of Bill Evans, with many silences offering space between chords and plenty of chromatic chordal color.

As Long As I Live is another light love song, but on this one, Diana's delivery is fresh rather than world weary, although it still has all the humor of the earlier songs on the album. Diana delivers a fleet piano solo full of rhythmic drive. Diana certainly serves this tune up in rapid vocal style without missing a syllable. Ray Brown, as the former husband of the first lady of jazz, Ella Fitzgerald, ought to know about such things. In the manner of a teacher, he sagely notes Diana's "nice phrasing" and her "excellent" enunciation.

On The Sunny Side Of The Street, the twelfth track included on the 2000 release, was presumably recorded along with the rest of the album in 1993. One of those happy exhortatory tunes where optimism is unflagging in the face of every kind of adversity, the song is delivered with a nice combination of swinging insouciance and happy humor. Diana's voice is strong, almost muscular.

Jim West of Justin Time says he cannot remember exactly

how many copies of the first issue of this album were released. He thinks about 3000. In any case, the album has been re-released several times following each of Diana's successes, and in 2001 it was awarded status as a gold record in Canada, as many of Diana's new fans bought the old record to catch up on her catalog. Perhaps the best thing about listening to this album is the experience of hearing an entirely different approach from her most recent albums. It's a pleasure to play these different albums one after another and observe the development of an artist who is constantly evolving from one album to the next.

———

Diana Krall's second album, ONLY TRUST YOUR HEART, was recorded on the GRP label, a subsidiary of the Verve Music Group, itself a subsidiary of the media and entertainment conglomerate associated with Universal Studios in Hollywood. The label claims that it "became synonymous with great contemporary jazz in the mid-80s. The genre called 'smooth jazz' has now grown up — and GRP is the home to many of its brightest stars." As a performer with this label, Diana begins to appear in excellent musical company. The outstanding guitarist George Benson and the leading male jazz singer Al Jarreau are two well-known musical performers who have appeared on GRP.

The entire presentation of this album seems to announce that the producers are fully aware that they have a rising star on their hands. The photographs of Diana in the album booklet reflect a new effort to create an intriguing persona for this performer. To charges that she has become a record label creation, Diana claims that she has exercised control over the image-making on her albums, including suggesting the kind of photographs required and choosing her own wardrobe for the photo shoots. Whoever constructed the image this album booklet presents, it is a smart and a canny one, responding both to Diana's background as a jazz neophyte and student, and to her future possibilities as a glamorous, fully self-confident professional. The image is ladylike and sensual.

She is shown on the cover of the booklet in a slightly out-of-focus photograph of her head and upper torso, with her head thrown back, eyes closed, running her hands through her hair, a posture at once sensual, meditative, and inviting.

The 'centerfold' of the booklet is produced in the style of a 1940s movie poster. Diana leans with her right hand on a column made up of the letters of her own name printed in a dusty rose color running up the side of the page. The actual photograph, like all the other photos in the booklet, is in black and white. Diana is wearing a long, elegant black gown in a heavy, wintry fabric, with buttons running from hem to neck. Her head, framed in a long sweep of blond hair, is turned in full profile, and her left hand is laid elegantly on her breast in a gesture that seems mildly self-protective, but also slightly histrionic and provocative. Leaning slightly backwards, away from the direction of her gaze, her posture suggests both interest and cool scepticism toward the subject of her gaze, and perhaps a hint of mild shock and mock withdrawal. The overall effect is of the cool glamor of a screen goddess of 1940s *film noir* ambience, the star whose smooth blond hair covers one of her eyes —Veronica Lake, perhaps, or Lauren Bacall. The booklet also features apparently candid black and white photographs of the musicians in the band, featuring Diana casually posing with Stanley Turrentine and consulting with Ray Brown in the midst of the recording session in her role as aspiring student.

The name of Tommy LiPuma appears on the album cover as producer, marking the first instance of a fruitful creative collaboration that has continued through each of the albums Diana has produced since. She is once more surrounded by the very finest of musicians. Ray Brown himself plays bass on four tracks, joined on three of them by the veteran tenor saxophonist Stanley Turrentine. The album booklet notes that "Diana was asked to suggest other ideal players for her album, and she said immediately, 'Stanley Turrentine' — and she got him!" It is no surprise that Turrentine would appear on an album with Ray Brown. In an interview on NPR, Turrentine reveals his long-time hometown connections with Brown and other Pittsburgh musicians: "I'd come home from school and Ahmad Jamal would be sitting at the piano — at our piano practicing. I used to sit at home and Ray Brown used to deliver our paper on Thursdays, the *Pittsburgh Courier.*"

Stanley Turrentine appeared often on the legendary Blue Note label during the 1960s, where he was heard with Horace Parlan, Art Taylor, Jimmy Smith, Duke Jordan, Horace Silver, Duke Pearson, and Kenny Burrell. As one critic has commented, "what first leaps out and grabs the listener's attention is Turrentine's sweet yet muscular sound, which suggests Johnny Hodges more than the classic Swing tenors. A flexible voice, it can deepen to a resonant honk, soar into one of the most piercingly full-throated cries in jazz, and broaden to a thick, sensuous vibrato on ballads. Turrentine tends to play on top of the beat, making for a deep, trancelike groove, and his phrasing draws on both modern jazz and R&B." The presence of Turrentine's sax on this album seems to add the richness and warmth of another human voice singing and speaking on top of Diana's voice and the sound of the rhythm section. For me, at least, Turrentine's saxophone gives rise to a wish to hear Diana sing more often with the sound of horns behind her, the interplay of different voice-like sounds so typical of the best of the classical jazz singers.

On five of the tracks, Diana is joined for the first time on record by the young bassist Christian McBride, who is described in italics in the album notes as the *"Future* of the bass," with Ray Brown acknowledged as "the *Master.*" The album notes refer to the many bassists who have played a role as Diana's mentors — Bryan Stovell, Don Thompson, John Clayton, and Ray Brown. "They are my left hand," Diana notes. "My bass mentors are truly my teachers. They have been the voice of leadership and experience, and I have learned so much music from them."

Christian McBride has been touted by *Time* magazine as "the most promising and versatile bassist since Charles Mingus," high praise indeed for a 23-year-old artist. McBride's talents were first recognized by Wynton Marsalis, who invited McBride as an eleventh-grader to join him on stage during a visit to Philadelphia's High School for Creative and Performing Arts, where McBride was studying bass. McBride later went on to Juilliard to study classical bass, but "hung up" his classical bass career to play jazz. He has performed since on more than 70 albums, with the likes of Joe Henderson, Etta Jones, Wynton Marsalis, Bruce Hornsby, Pat Metheny, Cyrus Chestnut, Benny Green, Joshua Redman, and the wonderful singer once known as Betty Bebop, Betty Carter.

The fourth member of the band is drummer Lewis Nash. Nash was the regular drummer between 1990 and 2000 with the trio of the master jazz pianist, Tommy Flanagan. He has played with Dizzy Gillespie, Oscar Peterson, Ron Carter, the Don Pullen/George Adams Quartet, Sonny Rollins, Stan Getz, Art Farmer, Clark Terry, and Milt Jackson. His credentials also include an appearance on the Grammy-award winning *Look What I Got* by Betty Carter.

The album begins with a spirited rendition of the humorously named *Is You Is Or Is You Ain't My Baby*, written by Billy Austin and Louis Jordan. Diana's rich contralto is complemented by deft accompaniment from Turrentine, who also performs a sweetly singing solo and a couple of warm saxophone breaks.

The next song on the album is the title tune, *Only Trust Your Heart*, which begins with Diana's piano in a meditative mood.

> Never trust the stars
> When you're about to fall in love
> Look for hidden signs before you start to sigh
> Never trust the moon
> When you're about to taste his kiss
> He knows all the lines and he knows how to lie ...
>
> – BENNY CARTER/SAMMY CAHN

Her wistful vocal is matched by an equally dreamy piano solo, evoking lost, false, even unwanted love in a mood of deep melancholy. The song seems to say that in spite of doubt, uncertainty, and sadness in love, including the definite possibility of betrayal, it is important only to "trust your heart," a constant theme in all the work of Diana, who claims to approach her art mainly from an emotional rather than a cerebral direction.

Diana's rendition of a Peggy Lee number, *I Love Being Here With You*, represents a complete change of mood, from the slow, restrained melancholy on the previous tune, to an upbeat happiness and delight. Giving testimony to her ability to evoke varied moods, Diana enters the mood of a happy and friendly love with a swift elan. Her own piano and Turrentine's warm asides contribute to a swinging happy atmosphere.

This light and happy mood carries through to Diana's treatment of *Broadway*, a song obviously celebrating the New York avenue which is the symbol of the American stage. As a New York resident now since 1990, Diana seems to reflect on her experience in the city, her delight in its rich life and history.

Broadway, Broadway
Everybody's happy and gay
Where the night is brighter than day
Up along Broadway . . .

Broadway,
Take a little time out to play
Where the joy of living holds way
Up along Broadway
— BILL BYRD/TEDDY MCRAE/HENRI WOODE

Diana's appreciation for the work of tastefully melodic drummers is reflected once again in the relaxed solo delivered by the subtle brushwork of Lewis Nash.

On the next song, Diana returns to a lyrical mood. *Folks Who Live On The Hill* is a poetic treatment of a little-heard Jerome Kern and Oscar Hammerstein tune from the 1937 film called *High, Wide And Handsome*, featuring Irene Dunn. Ostensibly a tune about the happiness of a married couple who contemplate a future life ensconced comfortably on a hill with their family, Diana's meditative vocal and piano playing unaccountably evoke a feeling of melancholy and absence, not entirely appropriate perhaps to the overt meanings of the lyrics, but somehow convincing, anyway.

Another happy tune follows, the well-known and often performed standard, *I've Got The World On A String*. McBride contributes a vocal-type plucked solo following a brisk, good-humored and swinging piano solo by Diana. Diana's voice is gritty and gutsy throughout.

In performing the Duke Ellington composition *Squeeze Me*, Diana delivers a combination of sensual dreaminess and a swinging light funk. The song provides Diana with an opportunity to showcase her growing ability to display a wide range of differing though related emotions in the course of a single song, as she moves through the yearning to the playful, to the wistful, to the sensual.

> Treat me sweet and gentle
> When you hold me tight
> Just squeeze me
> But please don't tease me
>
> I get sentimental
> When you hold me tight
> Come and squeeze me
> But please don't tease me ...
>
> – DUKE ELLINGTON/LEE GAINES

All Night Long, a quiet love song delivered in Diana's whispered mode, is about dreaming of an absent lover. It's hard to tell whether the song is addressed to a close confidante, or is more in the form of internal dialog, a song to oneself.

> Never knew the softness of his tender kiss
> Don't know if he's weak or strong
> All I know is that he's every dream I dream
> All night long

Never heard him say a single word of love
Don't know his fate or his soul
Cause he only speaks to me in dreams I've dreamed
All night long

When I sleep he tells me he's in love with me
And how much he needs me to be near
But at best my dreams is just a fantasy
If I touch his hand he'll disappear ...

— CURTIS LEWIS

An extended piano solo and a series of piano breaks in a slow and evocative blues mode contribute to a mood both dreamy and melancholy. The piano work in its precise timing of silences and the mallet work of the drummer recall the rhythmic atmosphere of one of Diana's major influences, the pianist Ahmad Jamal.

The album ends with *CRS Craft*, a bright and bluesy instrumental featuring Stanley Turrentine and a typically swinging solo from Diana, playing in her driving mode.

Diana has remarked ruefully on her vocal performance on this album, saying that listening to it today is "not painful" but "torturous." Even if there are some instances where Diana reaches for vocal effects that the limitations of her voice will not allow, there is too much of real jazz value, too much warmth and spirit, and too much vocal sensitivity to dismiss it so completely. There's no question that by trying to do too much, Diana sometimes seems to lose control of some of these songs, sounding a touch artificial and affected, losing the sense of sincerity which is the basic hallmark of her best vocals. But the failures and shortcomings of this album are the result of trying to do too much. Diana is testing and stretching her capabilities, rather than sticking with the safe and sure. By testing her limits, Diana is able to find her real terrain, to step out with a more secure sense of where her best talents lie. With her next album, she begins to find her feet.

I'm An Errand Girl For Rhythm, the first song on Diana Krall's third album, ALL FOR YOU, begins with the words, "Here's something that I'd like to bring to you, all wrapped up in cellophane, designed for you." The words seem to underline one of several meanings implied by the title. First, the idea that the contents of the album are delivered as a gift to an appreciative audience, a CD wrapped up in cellophane. The album is also a tribute to the music of Nat King Cole, dedicated to the "Nat King Cole Trio." Then, too, the album name contains a possible third meaning — an offer of love from the dramatic persona of the singer to an imaginary lover. Taken together, these meanings combine to make the album into a complete offering, a gift to the world.

The songs on the album are all drawn from the *ouevre* of the famed Nat King Cole Trio, first recorded on Capital records for an entire decade, beginning in 1943. The album notes on *All For You*, composed by Jerry Teachout, remark on the existence of two different Nat King Coles, one well-known, the other now all but forgotten except by real jazz aficionados. First, "the balladeer with the taffy-rich voice," who sang the popular favorites still so often heard today: *Unforgettable, Nature Boy, Mona Lisa, Sweet Lorraine*. And second, the "forgotten Nat King Cole," who was "one of the three or four best pianists in the history of jazz, a deceptively easygoing virtuoso whose crystalline solos and dead-center swing left their mark on a hundred distinguished admirers, including Oscar Peterson and Bill Evans."

"I've listened to Nat Cole since I was 12 years old," Diana remarks, "sometimes on a daily basis. His trio influenced all of the people I've admired and learned from, like Oscar Peterson, Bill Evans and Ahmad Jamal. Nat Cole is all over pretty much everything I do." Elsewhere she has commented that Cole has been a "major, major influence. Everything is great, but I particularly like the *After Midnight* sessions. He's two people. He's a great pianist on his own, and he's a great singer. The way he'd interpret a lyric — swinging, relaxed; the way he'd use guitar in a trio. Arrangement wise he was a huge influence, too. I have the Mosaic boxed set, all the Capitol recordings. He interests me as a jazz pianist as well as a singer, equally, and I think if he didn't sing he'd still be one of the most important jazz musicians."

The album cover and its booklet represent a movement toward greater simplicity, away from the outrightly glamorous presentation of Diana on her previous album. The front of the booklet, which doubles as the front cover of the CD album, features Diana seated unpretentiously at the piano bench, wearing a simple black skirted outfit, leaning slightly forward with her arms crossed and resting on her crossed legs. Her glance is an intriguing mixture of challenge and friendly appeal. The back cover of the album features a pensive Diana in full profile, barefoot and wearing a casual gray sweatshirt and a pair of blue jeans, looking for all the world like a young woman who works in an office relaxing in the bright sunshine of a window seat enjoying her day off.

There are four other pictures of Diana in the booklet, along with thumbnail photographs of the two other musicians in her trio. The inside cover of the booklet contains a high contrast black and white photo in which only Diana's face and hair emerge from a uniform black background. Her posture might indicate that Diana is hunched over the piano keyboard, prepared to begin playing, and has cast a glance over her shoulder, perhaps looking for someone in the audience before beginning to play. The look and posture is smoky and passionate, slightly startled-looking, and again, slightly challenging — it evokes the romantic *film noir* look of the jazz nightclub *chanteuse*, an aura of mild disenchantment and experience. A second photograph in the booklet is highly enigmatic. Again in black, Diana is seated at a table underneath a poster printed in French advertising "waffles dry and filled" (*gaufres, seches et fourree*). There is something chaste, pre-Raphaelite in the *chiaroscuro* of the photo and in Diana's gaze, the image of a young woman waiting to be joined by someone important in her life, a lover perhaps, a new and exciting acquaintance. It is obviously a cosmopolitan, urban image, and it might have been taken in any one of half a dozen cities in North America. The words in French on the poster suggests Paris or Montreal, though in today's world of interchangeable cosmopolitan images, the actual venue might easily be New York or even Vancouver. A supplementary photograph shows Diana, differently dressed, seated at a restaurant table in front of a venetian blind. The dazzling light from the exterior casts Diana's face and seated body into shadow. One can barely make out the main features of her face — she becomes anonymous, another working woman alone in a city. A jacket thrown over the empty chair beside an empty space on the table suggests a woman alone, expecting no one, calmly stirring her coffee or tea. Taken together, these images seem to represent a young woman in command of herself and her own life, confident, self-possessed, and fully self-directed, but nonetheless modest and unassuming.

In emulation of the original Nat King Cole Trio, Diana has chosen the format of the drummerless trio, featuring bass, guitar, and her own piano. This simple format requires a very tight musical discipline on all of the performers. Without the steady percussive sound of the drums, it is easy to lose the beat and hence the coherence of any song. But the absence of the drummer provides for a lighter, freer sound, and more rhythmic flexibility.

Diana appears for the first time on this album with her own performing trio. The personnel for her two previous CDs were put together only for the recording sessions, and although Diana had played individually and in some cases collectively on some occasions with the other instrumentalists, she had never previously entered the recording studio with a regular working band. Diana had already been performing for an entire summer with the band that went with her into the recording sessions for ALL FOR YOU. The liner notes enthusiastically comment that "this group is as tight as the wedding ring on a fat man's finger."

And it is. Diana is accompanied by the guitarist Russell Malone and the bass player Paul Keller. The excellent young pianist, Benny Green, sits in on *If I Had You*. Percussionist Steve Kroon plays bongos on *Boulevard Of Broken Dreams*. The album showcases Diana's fruitful association with the tunefully elegant guitarist Russell Malone. Malone says he was impressed with Diana's vocal and interpretive accomplishments months before he met her in person. He said he was driving home in 1994 from the supermarket when he heard Diana singing *All Night Long* from her second album. His response, according to an interview in *Saturday Night*, was "Holy Smoke!" He soon joined the trio.

The album contains a marvelous mixture of different kinds of songs taken from the Nat King Cole songbook: there are humorous and suggestive novelty tunes, melancholy tunes of lost love and lost hope, dreamily romantic tunes, and songs of joyous love. One cannot escape the impression that Diana was striving to recreate her own pleasure and delight as a teenager, listening and re-listening to these songs, absorbing every musical and emotional nuance.

The title and presentation of the first song on the album, *An Errand Girl For Rhythm*, appears almost as a mission statement on Diana's part.

If you want to swing and shout
Get your heels and get about
I'm an errand girl for rhythm, send me

Just get hip and follow through
I'll deliver straight to you
I'm an errand girl for rhythm, send me . . .

    — NAT KING COLE

Diana Krall is an errand girl for rhythm. She exercises her talent for charmingly suggestive humor on a tune written by Nat King Cole himself. Following a short vocal chorus by Diana, Russell Malone contributes a boppy guitar solo, in turn followed by a piano solo in Diana's best Oscar Peterson, Errol Garner swinging style. Diana then delivers a vocal chorus featuring sudden changes in tempo, followed by some humorous vamps on piano and guitar, evoking the corny swing of previous eras. The timing in this good-humored novelty piece is smart throughout.

The original model of *Gee Baby, Ain't I Good To You* was recorded by the Nat King Cole Trio on October 11, 1942. Nat's voice on this piece is lighter and less all-embracing than his later work once he had stopped playing piano in the 1950s. The guitar solo by Oscar Moore shows a heavy influence of the style of Django Reinhardt, whose stylings, along with those of Charlie Christian, revolutionized the playing of the jazz guitar. Cole's references to the expensive gifts of a fur coat, diamond ring, and a Cadillac given to a female lover seem to be delivered without any hint of irony, although the lyrics suggest that the singer is engaged in an argument with his lover, explaining the reasons why he deserves to be better loved on account of such fine gifts, so generously given as the sign of "being good" to his lover.

> Love makes me treat you
> The way that I do
> Gee baby, ain't I good to you . . .
>
> Bought you a fur coat for Christmas
> Diamond ring
> Big Cadillac car and everything
> What makes me treat you
> The way that I do
> Gee baby, ain't I good to you
>
> — DON REDMAN / ANDY RAZAF

In Diana's version, the presence of her suggestive female voice introduces a teasing note of irony, especially in the references to the luxurious and expensive gifts. Her emphasis on the words "and everything" at the end of the list of gifts seems to bring in a note of doubt, regret, perhaps even shame at the female character's acquiescence within this relationship. A social barrier is being transgressed here: instead of a man with ample economic means showering a woman with expensive gifts, the equation is reversed. The woman in this relationship is the well-heeled one, the one who buys her man the fur coat, the diamond ring and the Cadillac. At the very least, we are dealing with people who live outside conventional values and the ritual of conventional romantic courtship. Diana's suggestive treatment of the lyrics manages to convey a definite, if only implied irony, shaming the lover for his ingratitude for all the gifts he has received without offering any repayment in the form of returned love and faithfulness.

Russell Malone's slow, bluesy guitar intro, like Oscar Moore's on the Nat King Cole version, evokes the playing of Django Reinhardt, though differently and indirectly, mostly in the way the final notes in some of his phrases are turned, artfully suggesting Django's style, without simply mimicking it. Malone's guitar introduction is followed by a piano solo in slow blues mode, swingy and seductive. Diana's first vocal entry appears as a kind of pleasant surprise. In these early records, Diana has a way of jumping into the music with razor sharp timing, the sudden injection of a new driving element. Malone delivers some high octane traditional slow blues licks, and so does Diana, and again her vocal reappears with a sudden spring, yet so smoothly and accurately in terms of its timing that it seems to arrive as a completely natural extension of the instrumental music that precedes it.

Nat King Cole's version of *You Call It Madness (But I Call It Love)* was recorded on May 1, 1946. A typical love song of the period, sweet, dreamy, delivered in a soft and pleading voice, the song suggests, in its attitude to unanswered love, an infidelity on the part of the absent lover, who has callously treated the love relationship as a mere "plaything."

> I can't forget the night I met you
> That's all I'm dreaming of
> And now you call it madness
> But I call it love
>
> You made a promise, to be faithful
> By all the stars up above
> Now you call it madness
> But I call it love . . .
>
> — GLADYS DUBOIS/CON CONRAD/RUSS COUMBO/PAUL GREGORY

While Nat's version of the song begins abruptly with his warmly pleading vocal, Diana's version begins with a short instrumental introduction. Cole's version suggests a direct face-to-face personal appeal to his lover, who is actually present in the flesh. By contrast, Diana's quiet, near whisper suggests a late night telephone call from the rejected lover to the absent one, though the words could also be the content of a letter. Diana's breathy vocal treatment suggestively conveys not an attitude of anger toward the lover's betrayal, but regret, pleading, soft cajoling, a sad and tender reproach.

This is the second time that Diana has recorded *Frim Fram Sauce*, reflecting her own enjoyment of the song as much as a desire to 'get it right', even though a song of this kind might be performed in several different ways, each of them 'right' in its own way. The Nat King Cole Trio recorded one of several different versions of the song on October 11, 1945. Diana's first version can be heard on STEPPING OUT, recorded in 1993. Her voice on this second version is much smoother and more sweetly good-humored than the previous one, and in that sense closer to the original Nat King Cole version. The listener receives a strong impression that every phrase of this version has often been rehearsed, the whole presentation carefully crafted. Compared to her own previous version of the song, Diana's voice is smoother, less urgent, more relaxed. There is vocal confidence in every phrase, reflecting Diana's increasing mastery of her vocal instrument.

Of course, the way that Diana delivers the song, it is about more than food. At first the delicacies named in the song sound like staples of spicy New Orleans Cajun cooking, but no glossary of Cajun or New Orleans cookery provides a definition, much less a recipe, for frim fram sauce, or the mysterious sha fa fa, either.

I don't want french fried potatoes, red ripe tomatoes
I'm never satisfied
I want the frim fram sauce
With ausenfay and sha fa fa on the side . . .
    – JOE RICARDEL/REDD EVANS

In several different printed versions of the lyrics, "frim fram" is always spelled the same way, but some of the other words are rendered differently in various printed versions. The last word in the chorus, for example, is alternatively rendered "ausenfay" or 'Aussen Fay." In one version of the lyrics, these words are 'translated' into an understandable English phrase, "awesome taste," which sounds nothing at all like either Nat's or Diana's actual pronunciation of the word. The side dish is alternatively rendered in different printed versions of the lyrics as "sha fa fa," "shifafah," "chefafa," and even "chabopa." The liner notes for one of Nat's album compilations (Mosaic) suggest a precise geographical reference — an Ausen bakery that served something called "chefafa" on the side. A good-humored debate has broken out among some of Diana's fans about whether these are really meaningful words at all or simply nonsense syllables.

One fan points out that Diana's version of *Frim Fram Sauce* omits a tagged aside that appears on all of the existing Nat King Cole versions. On the Nat King Cole version, after the final words of the song, and also following a brief instrumental coda, Cole is heard speaking, rather than singing, the words, "Now, if you don't have it, just bring me a check for the water."

By omitting these final words, Diana puts a different spin on the song, which turns the reference to fake menu items in Cole's version into something else entirely, metaphorically linking a hot meal with a sensually hot time.

> . . . Well you know a girl
> She really got to eat
> And a girl she should eat right
> Five will get you ten
> I'm going to feed myself right tonight
>
> I don't want fish cakes and rye bread
> You heard what I said
> Waiter please, I want mine fried
> I want the frim fram sauce
> With ausenfay and sha fa fa on the side

Boulevard Of Broken Dreams is one of the most beautifully sorrowful songs in all of Diana's work. Her presentation of this Al Dubin and Harry Warren composition lends the song a European or Continental feeling of deep loss and disenchantment, as well as more than a hint of mournful decadence. The original tune was written in 1933 and included in the 1934 Hollywood movie *Moulin Rouge*. In its melancholy, the song evokes the mood, the distant beauty, sadness, and wistful sophistication of a Marlene Deitrich or Greta Garbo. It is at once romantic and very sad. The dreamy, chordal piano introduction owes much to Bill Evans' influence with its elegant lyricism. With bongos in the background, the piano sets the mood for the rest of the song.

It is interesting to compare Diana's version of *Boulevard Of Broken Dreams* with the classical version produced by Tony Bennett for Capitol in 1950, his first hit record. Bennett's voice is brash and loud, a mood that is fortified by the brassy accompaniment, featuring the clacking of castanets. The tune is a tango, and on Bennett's version, the instrumental portion is done in exaggerated 'Latin' style. The effect is to place the singer in some way outside the action, outside the story, a detached observer rather than a full participant, an outsider making a comment on the sadness of the lives of the people who live on the boulevard of broken dreams.

Diana sings the song in a much softer and more suggestive style, creating a dreamy, almost hypnotic atmosphere of mystery. The singer herself appears not just as a detached observer of life on the boulevard of broken dreams, but as an actual resident of the boulevard, an actor, a full participant in the life there. In the song, a woman alone meets with an unknown other person, of indeterminate gender. In a voice and timbre both sinuous and hypnotic, she sums up the substance of her life, explains her presence: "I walk along a street of sorrow, the boulevard of broken dreams." The woman is the intimate and the observer of two other characters — the male Gigolo and the female Gigolette, named obviously for the profession they pursue, bestowing sexual favors in return for money. Or perhaps the singer herself is "Gigolette," commenting ruefully on her own life. The song sketches the lives of these two dramatis personae, who have become lost souls. In their worldly cynicism, they can easily "take a kiss without regret, so they can forget their broken dreams." The generic naming of the two characters, Gigolo and Gigolette, has the effect of introducing a kind of stagy melodrama containing both pathos and irony, a rag tag Charlie Chaplin element. The woman in the song confides, "Here is where you'll always find me, / always walking up and down. / But I left my soul behind me, / in an old cathedral town." Diana's vocal presentation imbues these lines with a sense of irreparable loss. By contrast, Bennett's version, with its brasher approach, provides space for a kind of detachment from the obvious terrors the lyrics suggest. But Diana's moody treatment allows no such release. The singer is implicated in the moral atmosphere of the song — and so is the listener. Diana's presentation hovers very close to the territory of real despair, even though she relaxes this mood in her vocalizations in the final verse so as to introduce a note of detached insouciance, flagging the song as really an elegant emotional fantasy, a sad melodrama with ironic overtones rather than a complete tragedy.

According to his own later comments, Tony Bennett regarded his treatment of the song as a social commentary, presumably on the American cultural phenomenon, typified by the Hollywood sensibility, involving the false promotion of fantastic images of riches and fame, sure to be disappointed and defeated. In a joint interview with Diana, Bennett notes, "It was my first recording. It was kind of a social statement when I sang it, because of all the people less fortunate in the world. The song just tells a story about the boulevard of instant dreams, and it was an instant hit." Diana's treatment of the song suggests not only the world of the hollow dreamers on Hollywood Boulevard, but the jet set world, where money, luxury, and privilege are won not by hard work or ability but through a kind of luxurious prostitution. These people have lost their souls, sad perhaps, but in the wider scheme of things, not that tragic.

Russell Malone's guitar playing is supremely sensitive to the mood on this song. His guitar, like Diana's voice, arrives in low register, mournful, full of regret and loss. Echoing the melody of the words, the guitar expands the musical field. The instrumental solos both on piano and guitar are like dramatic monologs, each unfolding a rich array of melancholy emotional color and nuance. Diana uses a very few carefully applied vocal distortions to deepen the emotional emphasis of some of the words. Performed with less taste and artfulness, these vocal distortions might easily be considered simple vocal tricks. Diana's way of stretching the syllables of some of the decisive words of the song, while pressing a melting emotional intensity into the final word of the line — for example in the verse, "The joy that you find here, you boooor-rrowwww!" — is entirely convincing. Equally convincing is the odd phrasing of the final repetition of the title words at the end of the song and her way of holding and fading the final word, "dreeeEEEeeem—s". The song ends with another complete piano solo, filled with rippling bass notes and an artful fade-out on quick figures played in the upper middle register, full of a shimmering array of effects, shifting accents and tempos. At six minutes and twenty-seven seconds, the song is almost twice as long as most popular songs, yet the song doesn't drag because of all the emotional and narrative complexity Diana loads into it — all the expressive drama of a short story, or a one act play.

Baby Baby All The Time is another intimate confessional song. The character Diana creates in the song addresses an unknown other person, probably another woman, since the speaker dares to be intimate and confidential. But perhaps, too, the song is a kind of prayer, addressed to a spiritual guide, perhaps the Christian Lord Himself. The first verse outlines a portrait of a very lovable male lover, curly-haired, sweetly-mannered, whom the singer has carelessly "pushed away." Now, in the midst of lonely days, nights and hours, she longs to hear him say, "Baby, baby, all the time," once again. The final verse begins with an invocation — "Lord I pray that you will listen to my plea. / Keep him close to you so that he'll come back to me" — a mildly blasphemous request, calling upon God himself, conventionally the representative of a purified and sexless kind of love, to protect and defend an obviously very secular, sensual and earthly kind of love. The words themselves remind the listener of the famed *St. Louis Blues*, and the musical presentation, with its warm, inviting swing, adds to this atmosphere.

Hit That Jive Jack is another sprightly novelty tune to which Diana brings an appropriately brisk vocal style. Her piano solo is swinging with touches of virtuosity, and so is Russell Malone's guitar solo, which again evokes Django Reinhardt and Charlie Christian. This is happy, up-tempo jazz, with mock barbershop quartet-type vocals delivered by the entire trio adding to the retro-hip fun of the nonsense lingo of the lyrics. The instrumentals on the final verse, combining the piano, bass, and guitar in a rollicking rapid movement, are a virtuoso exercise in clarity and deft musical speed. Great chops and great jazz taste from each of the musicians.

You're Looking At Me, another melancholy song, features an extended solo by Russell Malone. The point of the lyrics hinges on the subtle interplay of an imaginary situation where the persona of the singer appears in an unflattering light through the gaze of a former lover. She seems to reproach him for his own reproachful look, which she sees in his eyes as he looks at her after a relatively long separation.

> . . . Who was so childishly flattered?
> Thought she'd swept him off his feet
> Who woke to find her dreams shattered?
> Might I repeat
> Might I repeat for you
> Needn't strain your eyes
> To see what I want you to see
> That's right
> You're looking at me
> — BOBBY TROUP

The singer seems to say, if you see in me a damaged person, lost innocence, this is what *your* betrayal of my pure love has made of me. Once again, Diana finds hidden depth in the lyrics and uses the subtlety of her intonations to create the character of the betrayed lover with a fresh complexity and sensitivity.

Many of the songs on this album deal with the melancholy of failed love. *I'm Thru With Love* is no exception.

> I've locked my heart
> I keep my feelings there
> I have stocked my heart
> Like an icy Frigidair
> For I need to care for no one
> That's why I'm thru with love . . .
>
> — MOTY MELNECK/GUS KAHN/FRED LIVINGSTON

Diana brings to this song a meditative piano in the mode of Bill Evans, a subtle touch, deep harmonies, a minimalist approach in which each chord is made to count. Her singing style is intimate, conversational. Here, the mood is everything. In a way, the words are completely unnecessary, the timbre of the vocal and the accompaniment so completely create the mood, as Diana uses her artful phrasing in an almost instrumental way.

Diana Krall seems to build each of her albums as a complete presentation from beginning to end. Each song has its place in the atmosphere of the album, almost as if the album itself were a kind of performance. *'Deed I Do*, a happy love song, obviously appears as a mood-breaker, introducing a new and humorous note between two songs of lost love. The playful lyrics of Fred Hirsch and Walter Rose are accentuated by romping solos from both Diana and Russell Malone.

A Blossom Fell, a poetic evocation of love and betrayal, was one of Nat Cole's greatest hits in the 1950s, and the Cole version of this Howard Barnes / Harold Cornelius / Dominic John song is still played on easy listening stations to this day. Diana's version opens with bursts of lightly touched notes lyrically evoking the delicate movement of falling leaves and blossoms drifting in the air. Although her treatment of the song is influenced emotionally by Cole's original version, her intonation and rhythmic approach are completely different. Her voice is a secretive whisper: "I saw you kissing someone new beneath the moon," drawing out the half rhymes in the lyric "you," "new," "moon," and finally breaking out in deeply yearning voice: "I thought you loved me, you said you loved me."

Russell Malone's solo — sweet, melancholy, romantic — provides a moment of quiet reflection. Once again, Diana's voice carries that same note of regret and reproach, all the more effective for its quiet acceptance of an unhappy situation. Although resigned, the vocal quality is not entirely passive. The character within the song seems to emerge with a sense that her own morality, the faithfulness of her own love, represents a real victory over any cynicism that might be caused by the lying lover who has cruelly betrayed this pure love. All of these emotions are suggested by the flexibility of Diana's vocals.

One has the impression that Diana is trying to use her vocal effects to rescue the lyrics of *If I Had You* from their banality ("I could show the world how to smile, turn the gray skies to blue"). She seems to call attention away from the words toward the singing itself and the emotional intelligence behind the vocal technique. *If I Had You* is a bold effort, but not entirely successful, though Diana's voice is very seductive.

Diana Krall's treatment of *When I Grow Too Old To Dream*, a well-known and often-produced standard, is an example of her growing mastery of the piano and vocals. A light and conventional sounding swing piano introduction is followed by a vocal interlude in which Diana's phrasing, full of subtle surprises, draws out a wealth of varied and even contradictory emotions. The promise of warm memories contends with poignant feelings of loss.

When I grow too old to dream, I will have you to remember.
When I grow too old to dream, your love will live in my heart.
So kiss me my sweet, and so let us part.
When I grow too old to dream, your love will live in my heart . . .

— ROMBERG/HAMMERSTEIN II

Neatly playing off the piano parts with the vocal parts, Diana keeps the song moving along a track which is both graceful and bouncy. Diana has remarked that the task of playing the piano and singing at the same time is somewhat like patting your head while rubbing your belly. The final number in the set, *When I Grow Too Old To Dream* is a bittersweet farewell, a presentiment of rich memories.

ALL FOR YOU was "break out" album in terms of public acceptance and acclaim, but also in terms of providing Diana with a landmark in her own development as a vocal artist. "I think the Nat King Cole tribute was a real stepping stone for me," she comments, "in terms of realizing what I do — which is *not* to shout. I'm able to sing very quietly in this trio, and play with a sense of spareness and simplicity — just play what's necessary and not try to prove anything pianistically, not try to burn down the rafters." The album held steadily on the *Billboard* traditional jazz chart for nearly 70 weeks, earned a spot in the *New York Times* Top Ten Adult Pop Albums for 1996, and won Diana her first Grammy nomination in 1997 in the Best Jazz Vocal category. Together with the trio, Diana performed the album's repertoire on tour, most notably at the Montreal Jazz Festival, where the show garnered international critical attention.

For the first time, Diana Krall's name began to be mentioned in prominent national and international magazines. In *Time* magazine, David Thigpen commented, Diana Krall "first drew note last summer at the Montreal Jazz Festival, where, using the tug of her bluesy, mahogany-grained voice, she parlayed a handful of jaunty Nat King Cole Trio tunes into a set of languid, open-hearted meditations with unexpected emotional impact. Accompanying herself on piano, she also showed that she knows how to swing — pounding out driving, rock-solid rhythms with her trio; when she soloed, she created patterns of brilliant, light-fingered notes that evoked Cole's easy, vibrant style."

LOVE SCENES is the third of five albums Diana Krall has recorded with producer Tommy LiPuma, each more successful than the last. By any measure, Diana's relationship with LiPuma is unique in the recording industry today, a relationship which has seen the two co-workers, along with LiPuma's hand-picked crew of sound technicians, evolve from productions of the greatest simplicity in the trio format to extravagant productions involving more than 40 symphonic musicians.

The story goes that when LiPuma first heard STEPPING OUT, he wasn't smitten by her work, but when he later saw a videotape of Diana on a cable show, he decided on the spot to begin working with her. As head of GRP Records and a regular producer for Verve, LiPuma's credentials include the production of more than 130 albums, some of them by the finest musicians and vocalists in jazz and pop music in the last three decades. He has a reputation for producing the sound known as "smooth jazz," sometimes disparaged as a commercialization of jazz. LiPuma may be the inventor of the term. GRP openly declares itself as a "smooth jazz" label, and LiPuma has produced a three-volume set of records under this very title. He has also produced a novelty item, a compilation of work by "lounge" or "jive" jazz artists called HIPSTERS, ZOOTS & WINGTIPS: THE 90S SWINGERS, in which Diana's version of *Hit That Jive Jack* keeps company alongside items like *Mr. Daddy O* by Big Voodoo Daddy and *Mr. Zoot Suit* by The Flying Neutrinos.

A professional saxophone player himself, LiPuma started out as an A&R man with A&M Records. Before becoming head of GRP in the mid 1990s, he was Vice President of Jazz and Progressive Music at Warner Brothers, then Senior Vice President for Electra Records' A&R department. LiPuma's first gold record production was *Guantanamera* by the Sandpipers. LiPuma's production of George Benson's BREEZIN' won a Grammy for Best Album in 1976. The year WHEN I LOOK IN YOUR EYES was nominated in this category, Diana is quoted saying, "I think it's telling that the only other jazz record that won album of the year is George Benson and Tommy LiPuma produced that record as well." Other jazz vocalists he has produced include Shirley Horn and Anita Baker, as well as Barbra Streisand's album THE WAY WE WERE and Natalie Cole's UNFORGETTABLE album. Perhaps the crowning achievement of LiPuma's career was the production of two albums by Miles Davis near the end of his career, TUTU (May 8, 1989) and AMANDLA (October 25, 1990), where Davis worked in and around the big-band compositions of Marcus Miller, which provided his unique trumpet stylings with a new, fertile rhythmic atmosphere. These were major productions, involving as many as 20 musicians and a large staff of sound technicians. They were among the last tracks that Davis ever produced before his death in September 1991.

As LiPuma recalls working on LOVE SCENES, "We started by recording the rhythm section. Then we sent the tracks to John, and he worked on the arrangements. He worked with them until he knew how to conduct the orchestra to the tracks. The most important aspect is the groove — that's the reason I decided to do it this way. You need to get the correct feel and the tempo to get the right performance. It is a lot easier when you can concentrate on those things with only three or four people in a room rather than with 40 people in there. If the performance doesn't have the right feel, it won't matter how good the arrangement or the orchestra tracks are."

"Someone said to me," LiPuma continues, " 'THE LOVE SCENES album sounds so simple. What did you do?' I said, 'That is the trick.' It shouldn't sound difficult or complicated. You have to cast the right musicians and the right mixer. I have been working with [engineer/mixer] Al Schmitt since 1972. Nobody records acoustical instruments like he does. The ambience you set in the room is very important too. Without making it apparent, you set the right mood. You want the musicians to just lose themselves in the music and forget where they are.' "

"Tommy's like . . . he and his wife are like my New York parents," Diana notes. "We're very close, and if you listen to earlier records I'd done, it wasn't until ALL FOR YOU that I started feeling what I wanted to do. I think for a record company to allow you to grow publicly like that is a good thing."

The production values on LOVE SCENES, both in terms of the recording and the album presentation, are by far the most luxurious in Diana's career thus far. The photography, art direction, and design are attributed, respectively, to Rocky Schenk, Hollis King, and Isabelle Wong. Full copies of the lyrics for each song are framed, each in a different way by different art objects — a portion of a stained glass window, images of musical instruments and microphones, an allegorical rococo etching of three cherubic infants cavorting beside a crown which has quite obviously fallen from the head of the skull lying beside what looks like a painter's palette and brushes at the feet of the infants. Another song frame shows an art-nouveau statuette of a gowned female figure holding aloft a cluster of lights. Diana, in a leggy and barefoot full-length pose, also wearing a long flowing gown, is seen to gaze upwards at the statuette with her head curiously bent to one side. The atmosphere throughout is melodramatic, almost gothic, in its excess. This atmosphere of luxury and taste creates a setting for the music the album contains.

The paper album cover, a three-page foldout, and the 20-page album booklet feature eleven different photographs of Diana. Most of these photos are extremely glamorous cameo shots of Diana close up in soft focus, but there are also pensive individual photographs of guitarist Russell Malone and bassist Christian McBride and a shot of Diana in an affectionate arm-on-shoulder pose with her producer, Tommy LiPuma. Diana is presented with all the style of a film goddess, appearing elegantly dressed amidst elaborate backgrounds of cupids, statuary, mosaics, and stained-glass windows. Diana is not smiling in these photographs, projecting her signature expression, which some critics have described as a "sullen goddess persona."

Yet in another small photo, Diana wears ordinary slacks and a blouse, in a homely snapshot-type pose, while another portrays a small blond girl, presumably Diana at the age of four or five, wearing a little girl's dressy Sunday frock, white knee socks, and a pair of patent leather shoes with a thin black strap across the ankles, smiling, as if to remind us that this goddess has human origins, and was once a young girl, living an ordinary life in an ordinary suburb with an ordinary family with ordinary feelings.

The photographs, then, are a fantasy — one might say "nothing more than a fantasy," but this would miss the point. Fantasy is above all what this album is actually about, a poetic fantasy involving the working out of the relationship between ideal notions of love and the common experience of love. In a written introduction to the album, evocatively printed in white ink on a gray background of alabaster statuary, Diana states her own poetic motives. "The songs are indeed about romance," she admits. "But to me there is a broader and more personal attachment to each of the songs than the standard definition of romantic love might imply. I think that these songs represent the strength of love, including the love of family and friends." Diana then invites her listeners to imagine their own "personal 'love scenes' among the mountains, oceans, rain and gardens of these songs." Diana's remarks have a special poignancy in the light of the fact that her mother, Adella, had recently been diagnosed with multiple myelar cancer and was undergoing the first of many treatments. Diana was prompted to "a look back at home, at the strength of all kinds of love, at what's important to me."

Because her mother was ill, Diana came to the studio feeling down, Tony LiPuma recalls, and chose from a long list of possible songs, a set weighted toward minor keys. They felt the mix would be too dark, and went back into the studio, where they settled on a different balance of moods. "I have a personal attachment to these songs," Diana says of the final selections for LOVE SCENES. "I picked 13 I liked and unconsciously, there's a lot of what I grew up with in them — the gardens, and rain and mountains and ocean."

Once again, Diana is working in the trio format with Russell Malone, ever sensitive to the shifting moods of her vocals, and Christian McBride. *All Or Nothing At All*, the first track on LOVE SCENES, opens with a brief bass introduction by McBride, which sounds like a Charles Mingus introduction as the bass comes forward as though enunciating words in an announcement. McBride and Diana carry on a short musical dialog, bass notes trading for Diana's soft alto. More and more, Diana is beginning to use her voice as an instrument in the manner of the classical jazz singers like Billie Holiday. By paying special attention to the sound of the words and artfully working their phrasing, she is able to extend the possibilities of their meaning within a multiple array of emotions.

Peel Me A Grape, a song many commentators and fans take as her signature work, places the luxurious tone of the album cover in comic, even ironic relief. Adopting the role of a spoiled *femme fatale*, a 'kept woman' who keeps her lover or sugar-daddy wrapped totally around her finger, Diana creates an amusing drama. The lover is helpless in face of the outrageous demands she makes.

Peel me a grape, crush me some ice
Skin me a peach, save the fuzz for my pillow
Talk to me nice, talk to me nice
You've got to wine and dine me . . .

Here's how to be an agreeable chap
Love me and leave me in luxury's lap
Hop when I holler, skip when I snap
When I say, 'do it,' jump to it

Send out for scotch, call me a cab
Cut me a rose, make my tea with the petals
Just hang around, pick up the tab
Never out think me, just mink me
Polar bear rug me, don't bug me
New Thunderbird me, you heard me
I'm getting hungry, peel me a grape

— DAVE FRISHBERG

The *femme fatale's* demand for material comforts and extravagant gifts is suggestively linked to ideas of sensual gratification with every *double entendre* phrase. The key to the erotic power of the song lies in the continued teasing of the lover's desires, putting them off with one request after another, while at the same time holding out the promise of a sensual reward in the end. Diana's suggestive voice weaves its way around this erotic terrain with sophisticated humor.

Throughout several months of 2001, television viewers in Canada often saw a clip of Diana performing the first few bars of *I Don't Know Enough About You*, created to advertise the forthcoming *Diana Krall in Paris* special. The words seemed to be addressed to Diana's audience, an invitation to get to know her better.

> I know a little bit about a lot of things
> But I don't know enough about you
> Just when I think you're mine
> You try a different line
> Baby, what can I do? . . .
> — PEGGY LEE/DAVE BARBOUR

On *I Miss You So*, the next track, Diana presents her most intimate and sensitive character, seductive, lyrical, full of restrained erotic suggestion. Her voice is like a whisper in the listener's ear, and the quiet solos by Diana and Russell Malone elaborate this mood perfectly.

The success of any singer in performing Ira and George Gershwin's *They Can't Take That Away From Me* depends upon the achievement of a subtle balance between the surface frivolousness of the words and the real feeling they conceal. The narrative of the song suggests a pair of lovers, who, for one reason or another, are unable to continue their relationship. The reasons for parting are not explicitly stated. The insouciance of the lyrics suggests that both lovers are worldly people, forced to separate by the demands of their respective lives. Diana's phrasing and intonation neatly frame each phrase, extracting a wide range of emotion.

The choice to include the song *Lost Minds* on this album represents a departure from Diana's usual repertoire of Tin Pan Alley standards or bossa novas. In her Bravo television feature, Diana comments that the choice of the song reflects her on-going fondness for the blues. Here, she chooses a blues tune by Percy Mayfield, sometimes referred to as the poet laureate of the blues, a singer and songwriter who wrote many songs for Ray Charles, including the highly popular *Hit The Road Jack*. Diana's version features a witty solo with some cool quotes by Russell Malone in the mode of the great blues player, Lightnin' Hopkins.

Diana gives *I Don't Stand A Ghost Of A Chance With You* a wistful treatment, which draws the listener in the deepest pangs of unrequited love. The song begins quietly with Diana's voice accompanied by tastefully unobtrusive slow guitar chords in the background. Diana sings this song much more slowly than other performers have done, and in a moodier, darker style. As she whispers the lyrics, she seems at times to be reaching into the bottom of her vocal register, singing at the limit of her breath, almost as if her voice will trail out completely.

Diana makes short work of *You're Getting To Be A Habit With Me*, approaching the song humorously in an up-tempo mode, providing an interlude between the melancholy mood of *I Don't Stand A Ghost Of A Chance With You* and *Gentle Rain*. A different sensibility is at work in *Gentle Rain* from standard North American treatments of romantic melancholy — a poetry drawn from the Latin or Spanish tradition of song-writing, drifting, transitory, fleeting moods. The vocal production is unique for Diana, hinting at the sound of Peggy Lee, perhaps.

Diana introduces *How Deep Is The Ocean (How High Is The Sky)*, this Irving Berlin classic, with a meditative ringing piano solo that leaves the listener wanting much more, until her voice takes over satisfyingly. The way she rags the last word "sky" of the second chorus is exciting, an evocative stylistic touch followed by an equally impressive piano solo, swinging and inventive from beginning to end, full of genuine feeling.

> . . . How far would I travel
> Just to be where you are?

How far is the journey
From here to a star?
And if I ever lost you
How much would I cry?
How deep is the ocean?
How high is the sky?

    — IRVING BERLIN

The snapping finger introduction to *My Love Is*, accompanied by the bass sounding like another human voice, recalls once again the vocalic imitations of Charles Mingus. Diana's vocal presentation recalls the sexy allure of Peggy Lee singing *Fever* as she performs this song completely without instrumental accompaniment other than the sound of her own snapping fingers and the bass. Her voice is conversational, funky and sensual throughout, at times filled with a hot, aching passion. Even without instrumentation, Diana's presentation swings almost enough to be actually danceable — a tribute to Diana's excellent sense of time and rhythm.

Garden In The Rain is another song evoking the British Columbia rainforest surrounding Diana's Nanaimo home. The lyrics, in their diction, their inversions of syntax, and their imagery of rain and gardens, suggest an Elizabethan love poem.

'Twas just a garden in the rain
Close to a little leafy lane
A touch of color 'neath skies of gray
The raindrops kissed the flowerbeds
The blossoms raised their leafy heads
A perfumed thank you
They seemed to say . . .

    — CARROLL GIBBONS/JAMES DYRENFORTH

The final chorus of this song is an example of one of Diana's stylistic trademarks: she sings in an open manner, with a pure, clear sound, balancing this against a harsher, more grainy style, in which she introduces a low register growl, mixing emotions of sweet purity with a funkier sensuality.

Diana deals with *That Old Feeling* in a similar vein to her treatment of *You're Getting To Be A Habit With Me*. The theme is at once the painful recognition of the transitory nature of love and the pleasurable memory of love, that "old feeling," a theme Diana has mastered, musically and emotionally.

After trying out a variety of vocal approaches on her first three albums, some less well adapted to the range and power of her voice and her own inner psychology, on LOVE SCENES Diana Krall has found her métier. With this record, she also solidified her reputation as one of the most commercially successful jazz artists of all time. LOVE SCENES sold more than 500,000 copies, and the record was certified Gold by RIAA on August 12, 1999. With this record, Diana succeeded in enhancing her artistry in the jazz trio format. Her sultry vocalization on *Peel Me A Grape* led some critics to remark that the song had "finally found its true voice" in Diana's presentation. LOVE SCENES also earned Diana another Grammy nomination for Best Jazz Vocal Performance in January 1998.

After producing four albums in the small group setting, Diana Krall embarks on a new musical adventure with WHEN I LOOK INTO YOUR EYES, singing for the first time on record in the context of a full orchestra. This album began to take shape when Johnny Mandel invited Diana to collaborate with him. "You may not know the name," Diana said in an interview while promoting WHEN I LOOK INTO YOUR EYES, "but you know the music. He wrote the theme to *M.A.S.H.*, he provided the arrangements for Frank Sinatra's RING-A-DING album. Johnny's also worked with Streisand and Tony Bennett. He's one of the greatest string arrangers out there." Diana fails to mention that Mandel is also one of the most innovative of all big-band jazz arrangers and composers, in the ranks of Billy Strayhorn and Quincy Jones.

Johnny Mandel began his composing career in the early 1950s, writing music for Latin bands and arranging the music for

Woody Herman's big band. In 1953, he was invited to join the Count Basie band as a trombonist and composer/arranger. Two of the tunes he wrote during his six month stint with Basie are part of the standard repertoire of big bands today, *Low Life* and *Straight Life*. Mandel made a significant contribution to the jazz tradition when in 1958 he wrote the score for the movie *I Want to Live*, a film starring Susan Hayward in one of her trademark roles as a "fallen woman," portraying Barbara Graham, the first woman ever executed in California, in a shocking and groundbreaking performance. The musical score was equally groundbreaking. Mandel's score was "the first film score that proved the emotional range that jazz could express," jazz writer Gene Lees has commented. The soundtrack of *I Want to Live* features the finest musicians from the West Coast school of cool jazz that flourished in the 1950s in Los Angeles. The band is led by baritone saxophonist Gerry Mulligan, with Art Farmer on trumpet, Shelley Manne on drums, Bud Shank on alto-saxophone, Frank Rosolino on trombone, Pete Jolly on piano, and Red Mitchell on bass.

Mandel introduced instrumentation never before heard in jazz — the contrabass clarinet, bass trumpet, bass flute and contra bassoon. At one stroke, he established himself as a daring new force, making a claim for jazz as a serious music capable of embracing social themes. The use of a jazz score in a major movie was a significant departure from the normal movie music of the time, which favored lush, semi-classical string productions. Mandel's score, with its brooding expressionist sound, introduced a new note of social realism in a film carrying a strong message against capital punishment.

Mandel went on to write songs for major singers like Dick Haymes, Hoagy Carmichael, Mel Torme, and Frank Sinatra, before returning to film and television scores. A list of his scores may appear as a surprise even to those who know his name: *Staying Alive* (with John Travolta); *The Verdict* (with Paul Newman); *Caddyshack* (with Chevy Chase and Bill Murray); *The Sailor Who Fell From Grace With the Sea* (with Kris Kristofferson and Sarah Myles); *The Last Detail* (with Jack Nicholson); *The Man Who Had*

Power Over Women; *That Cold Day In The Park*; *Point Blank*; *Pretty Poison*; *Harper*; *The Russians Are Coming, The Russians Are Coming*; *The Sandpiper*, *The Americanization Of Emily*, and *M.A.S.H.* He has also written music for contemporary recording artists Natalie Cole and Michael Jackson, while producing music for Manhattan Transfer, David Sanborn, and Shirley Horn on her 1992 Grammy winning record.

Impressed by her previous recordings, Johnny Mandel called Diana to compliment her. "Out of the blue," Diana recalls, "he called me up one day and said, 'Well, Diana, I just think you're the sweet spot on the baseball bat.'" Hearing this outrageously flattering compliment from the master, Diana says, "I almost dropped the phone." She adds, "I felt honored that Johnny wanted to work with me. That doesn't happen very often in somebody's lifetime. I had always thought it would be great to do something with strings, but it had to be the right person. And Johnny Mandel is certainly the right person. . . . I'm sure I'd heard Johnny Mandel since I was a baby with all the music that was in our house. So my first memory of Johnny Mandel was the composition, *Close Enough For Love*, and my first memory of meeting Johnny Mandel was in Los Angeles at a Jimmy Rowles celebration. Working with Johnny Mandel was one of the greatest experiences I ever had because I listened to all those records with Frank Sinatra and the arrangements he did for Shirley Horn and all the work he's done in the pop world . . . not to mention his compositions. So it was a bit intimidating at first because I think I was very much in awe of him. He tried to straighten me out with that by saying relax and it got to the point where we were working together, but . . . for someone like that you've got to be a little in awe."

Not overawed, though, for Diana kept her trio for the new album, adding Mandel's orchestrations as another instrument. "I hadn't thought of making an album with strings until Johnny Mandel called," Diana comments. "I still wanted to do more with my trio and a quartet setting, and I wasn't really comfortable with a complete switchover. So to me, this is the best of both worlds: the Diana Krall trio with Johnny Mandel orchestrating some of the tunes."

The album again features glamorous photographs of the star singer, juxtaposed with images of her as an ordinary young woman, on the cover and in the liner notes, all but one of them taken outdoors. These images evoke an entirely different feeling from the photographs in Diana's previous album LOVE SCENES, with its hint of romantic decadence. The feeling here is one of joy, delight, freedom, ecstasy.

Of the twelve songs on WHEN I LOOK INTO YOUR EYES, seven are accompanied by an orchestra playing arrangements written by Johnny Mandel. Diana plays once again with her old friends John Clayton on bass, Jeff Hamilton on drums, and Russell Malone on guitar. The ringing vibraphone of Larry Bunker adds to the sound of the strings and Diana's piano, bringing an extra shimmering suggestiveness. "There's no question that the strings shine a whole new light on some these tunes," Diana says. "I usually have a clear idea of what I want to do. We worked really hard on making sure all the parts fit together correctly. Really, it's a jazz group improvising as usual — the strings are just considered another instrument."

One of the means by which Diana and her musicians reinvigorate old songs is to place them in a new rhythmic environment. The repertoire of standards from the 1930s and 1940s is mostly made up of fox trots, the dance of choice during the 1930s and the 1940s, with their easy and relaxed 4/4 rhythm — slow, slow, quick, quick, as we used to repeat in our high school dance classes, learning the steps. Irving Berlin's *Let's Face The Music And Dance* has been performed by most of the masters of American pop music — most often by Fred Astaire, who made dance a metaphor for life, but also by Nat King Cole, Frank Sinatra, Tony Bennett, Ella Fitzgerald, Mel Torme, Anita O'Day, Sammy Davis Junior, and many others. Several commentators have remarked that Diana performs the song differently from anyone else. The lightly syncopated rhythms of the Argentine bossa nova played under the lyrics of this often-heard song helps to revive the music and lends the lyrics a fresh, contemporary feeling.

On Bob Dorough's *Devil May Care*, Diana uses her voice as

another musical instrument within the overall arrangement. Each solo within the trio format enters as part of a musical dialog, each making a point of its own. The music is lightly driving, forward moving, consistent with the message of the lyrics.

Live love today, love come tomorrow or may
Don't even stop for a sigh, it doesn't help if you cry
That's how I live and I'll die
Devil may care

— BOB DOROUGH

Diana's treatment of *Let's Fall In Love* invites comparison with the version by the 'incomparable' Ella Fitzgerald. Diana unquestionably follows the phrasing she learned from Ella, but her approach is much cooler and much quieter than Ella's warm, swingy treatment of the song. Ella is accompanied by some hot horn interpretations — trumpet, saxophone, and trombone — but Johnny Mandel's arrangement offers only a brief trumpet section punctuation, with the musical load carried mainly by Diana's piano, Russell Malone's guitar, and Larry Bunker's vibraphone stylings. All in all, a smoother, less jazzy presentation than Ella's, but no less satisfying.

The title song of the album, *When I Look In Your Eyes*, begins with a slow harp and vibraphone introduction, followed by a romantically sweet and sad string interlude. The guitar in solo mode introduces Diana's voice, which enters in her lowest register, almost at the point of breaking, going completely flat, almost spoken, rather than sung, followed by phrases sung in a slightly higher, sweeter register, balancing dark phrases against lighter ones. Diana fashions a unique emotional atmosphere, dark and melancholy, full of loss and sorrow: "When I look in your eyes / I see the sadness of a thousand goodbyes." When she intones "autumn comes, summer dies," this mood deepens to a level rare in American popular music. Diana uses her voice to suggest a serious engagement with life, almost philosophical. The poetic image at the center of the song, where the singer gazes into the eyes of her lover, discovering there not only the depth of her lover's personality and wisdom, but also the reflection of the entire world, is rich with affection.

> . . . Those eyes, so wise
> So warm, so real
> How I love the world, your eyes reveal
>
> — LESLIE BRICUSSE

The final phrase is beautifully rendered, the slurring of the final word is absolutely the right artifice to bring out the emotion. There are not many singers, past or present, capable of negotiating this kind of poetic depth and complexity of emotion without losing their bearings, and still fewer who dare to reach down to these depths of melancholy and find solace there.

Michael Franks' *Popsicle Toes* is a playful song dripping with *double entendre* and sexual innuendo: "Let's have a birthday party, you can wear your birthday clothes." Diana approaches the song with the appropriate sensuality in her voice, drawing out her phrasing to elicit the maximum sense of suggestion. She consistently adds a kind of musical lilt to each pronunciation of the word "toes," each time different, adding even more charm. The music is lightly funky and strongly blues-tinged.

There is something more than slightly menacing about the way Diana sings the old Cole Porter favorite *I've Got You Under My Skin*. The singer is determined to win the object of her affection using any means possible: "I would sacrifice anything come what might, for the sake of having you near." While these lines are usually delivered with humor and panache by other singers, Diana gives them the sound of a serious vow. And while "a warning voice that comes in the night" reminds the singer that the affair is impossible — "wake up to reality, don't you know you can't win," — the obsessed lover persists in the complaint, "I've got you under my skin." Repeated in slightly varied phrasings each time, this phrase seems to burrow like a parasite under the skin, a marvelous musical trope for the neurotic character of an obsessive and hopeless love. This love is dangerous, destructive. Diana's voice adds a threatening tone, which manages to suggest all of this without actually saying it. Such restraint is the mark of a true artist, nothing is overemphasized or overdrawn, only implied.

I Can't Give You Anything But Love again reminds the listener of Ella Fitzgerald. Ella's voice always suggested an unflagging innocence of approach to the world, a youthful, almost child-like quality, always fresh, and Diana's voice, in this song, echoes that feeling.

Most of the previous treatments of *I'll String Along With You* that I remember are breezy and light. The opening verses lend themselves to this treatment in a kind of tease — you're okay for the present, dear, but I'm still looking for my angel.

> You may not be an angel
> 'Cause angels are so few
> But until the day that one comes along
> I'll string along with you
>
> I'm looking for an angel
> To sing my love song to
> And until the day that one comes along
> I'll sing my song to you . . .
>
> – HARRY WARREN / AL DUBIN

But Diana chooses to introduce a deeper note of affection and devotion, emphasizing the third verse, and in this way provides an entirely new mood for the song.

> For every little fault that you have
> Say I've got three or four
> The human little faults you do have
> Just make me love you more . . .

Diana gives the George Gershwin and B.G. De Sylva song *Do It Again* an appropriately playful treatment. Well before the end of this song, we know that "it" alludes to something much more than simple kisses, as Diana slips in a sly note of raunchy humor at the end when she liltingly intones the words, "and again . . . and again . . . and again . . . and again . . . do it Aaaagaaain!"

Why Should I Care is designated as a "bonus track," separately produced by David Foster, courtesy of the Warner Music Group and Tommy LiPuma. This song was first featured in the introduction to Clint Eastwood's film, *True Crime*.

> Was there something more I could have done?
> Or was I not meant to be the one?
> Where's the life I thought we would share?
> And should I care? . . .
>
> Should I leave you alone here in the dark?
> Holding my broken heart
> While a promise still hangs in the air
> Why should I care?
>
> — CLINT EASTWOOD

The phrasing of the first few lines is drawn from the style of Frank Sinatra, but the intonation throughout is all Diana's own. She takes advantage of a variety of intonations on the question repeated at the end of each verse — Why *should* I care; Why should *I* care; Why should I *care* — to bring out the complexity of the emotions surrounding the parting of the lovers. In spite of the ironic tone of the lyrics, Diana presents a mood of true sadness. The listener is drawn irresistibly into the mood, which is sustained beautifully by the vocal notes of the saxophone solo and the all-embracing sound of the David Foster orchestrated strings.

The movie *True Crime*, a 1999 Warner Brothers release starring its director, Clint Eastwood, opens with a pre-credits series of shots of Diana singing Eastwood's *Why Should I Care?* The shot moves down from a position above Diana's head as she stands beside a grand piano wearing a simple black business suit that contrasts with her pale, ghostly countenance and her white-blond hair. This arresting image is a cameo in every sense of the word, outstanding for its purity and simplicity, emphasized by Diana's almost immobile posture. The image is intercut with shots from the film itself, impressionistically framing scenes from the break-up of the marriage of the irresponsibly unfaithful journalist who is the main character of the film — scenes of domestic disharmony, scenes of Eastwood chatting up a beautiful young woman in a bar — all moments later explained in the action of the film, the story of a Peter Pan character who discovers maturity in the midst of an effort to save the life of an Afro-American wrongly sentenced to death by lethal injection for a murder he did not commit.

The repeated refrain of the song — "Why should I care?" — comments upon the screen action, placing the action in a feminine perspective, commenting effectively on the damaging results of the main character's irresponsible behavior, his alcoholism, and his multiple marital infidelities, bringing to our attention the plight of his wife and daughter. Rather than projecting pathos, though, Diana's delivery of the lyrics unfolds a complex array of emotional perspectives between the male and the female characters, underlining a secondary theme of the film, the theme of forgiveness and redemption.

Clint Eastwood's directorial art succeeds in winding the opening cameo featuring Diana into the complete fabric of the film narrative. He also succeeds in presenting an arresting film image of Diana herself, the first of its kind. "Clint Eastwood told me, 'Don't do so much. Just stand there,'" Diana recalls her silver screen debut. Her appearance in Eastwood's film became the occasion for an outburst of gossip in the press. As Alison Kerr reported in the *Herald Magazine*, "Only a few weeks ago, her record company's London office was having a hard time persuading British newspapers and magazines to interview her about her forthcoming album. Then, out of the blue, the sultry Krall features were being splashed all over the tabloids, with headlines like 'Clint jazzes with singer half his age,' and 'Jazz girl at the center of Clint's marriage split.' Eastwood, already a known admirer of Krall's work, was reported to be pursuing their friendship to the detriment of his five-year marriage. Suddenly, the green-eyed blonde was hot property. The media were left to muse why the 36-year-old singer might forge what was described as an intellectual affinity with the 71-year-old film icon."

Diana Krall and Clint Eastwood had first met four years previously when Eastwood and his wife Dina came backstage after a concert. The basis of their friendship was their common passion for jazz. Eastwood's connection with the music goes back to his directorial debut in *Play Misty for Me*, a film about a jazz disc jockey stalked by a psychotic woman music lover, and he has also directed *Bird*, one of the only features about the life of jazz genius Charlie Parker. A frustrated jazz pianist himself, Eastwood has a particular affection for the instrument. Diana was reportedly awestruck with his knowledge of the music as he regaled her with stories of late jazz greats he has known. "Krall and Eastwood have never hidden the fact that they are good friends and that they enjoy spending time together at the piano," Alison Kerr continues." As far back as two years ago, Krall told the press: 'He and his wife and I like to hang out, and I play, and he plays.' " In *You* magazine, Adrianne Pielou quotes Diana as explaining, "I asked him if he knew anywhere I could go horse riding and he phoned up a friend who has a ranch. His daughter, Kimber, keeps her horses: she's become like a big sister to me — I actually see her more than him. When I'm in California I go to his house, play piano, hang out with his wife — we're the same age — and have dinner. Those rumors are getting tiresome and they sort of insult our friendship. But it's now given me a whole new appreciation for gossip, how it works. Elton [John] has been really helpful in that, though. He says as long as they spell your name right, you mustn't let yourself be upset by it. You've just got to laugh. I'm just amazed I was never linked with Bob Hope." In a *Toronto Sun* interview, Diana added, "They had me with Clint Eastwood one week, then they had me with Dustin Hoffman the next. I mean where's Brad Pitt and all these young guys? They've got me with all the old guys."

The gossip in the press was momentarily upsetting to a real relationship Diana was developing with scriptwriter John-Paul

Bernbach. He drank "two stiff gimlet cocktails before dinner when he heard the news," but they both came to see the funny side of this 'affair', as reported in *The Evening Standard*. "Flirty Harry!" Diana comments. "We thought, is this cool or terrible? But we survived it. I can always go home and snuggle up with John-Paul. I have an interesting and happy world. I don't care."

Diana's circle of film associates and acquaintances has expanded to include Dustin Hoffman, and she has also developed a close friendship with Lawrence Fishburne. She appeared on television's *Melrose Place*, where she played a jazz pianist in a bar, and on an episode of *Sex and the City*, while her music has been featured in another Eastwood film, *Midnight in the Garden of Good and Evil*, and in films with Robert DiNiro, Val Kilmer, and Danny De Vito. Diana has expressed an interest in becoming an actor, and to this end, she has taken several classes at the Actors' Studio in New York. But any dreams of becoming a star of the silver screen were subordinated to the production her next album, THE LOOK OF LOVE.

_____

Anyone who has seen the television special *Diana Krall in Paris* will have noticed the affection, if not the reverence, with which Diana Krall introduces Claus Ogerman on the stage of the Olympia Theatre, one of her collaborators in recording THE LOOK OF LOVE. "Claus Ogerman and Johnny Mandel have been my favorite arranger/composers since I was 17 years old," she says. "A long time ago, I'd mentioned possibly working with Claus to Tommy [LiPuma]. It seems as though I've been dreaming about it forever. I used to listen to the CITYSCAPE album he did with Michael Brecker almost every night when I was going to school at Berklee in Boston. But the possibility seemed very far away at the time. So when we saw the direction this album was taking, I started thinking about Claus again, and just imagining how great it would be if we could get him involved in the project."

The seeds of Diana Krall's sixth album go back to her teenage years, when she attended the Berklee College at the age of 17 and first heard the album CITYSCAPE, a collaborative work featuring the composer Claus Ogerman and the saxophonist Michael Brecker. Earlier she had likely listened to another Ogerman collaboration in Bryan Stovell's collection, the beautiful album, BILL EVANS TRIO WITH SYMPHONY ORCHESTRA, where Evans' lyrical piano stylings are framed by Ogerman's arrangements. She may also have heard the 1967 album FRANCIS ALBERT SINATRA AND ANTONIO CARLOS JOBIM featuring arrangements by Ogerman, and the 1977 original recording of Joao Gilberto's AMOROSO, with strings arranged by Ogerman, which included two tunes she would later record with Ogerman on THE LOOK OF LOVE, 'S Wonderful and Besame Mucho. Featuring a composition called The Presence And Absence Of Each Other, CITYSCAPES may have presented some musical solace for a young woman far from home living for the first time in a large city.

Diana and LiPuma began working on the album long before they made the decision to involve Ogerman, however. In fact, the vocal tracks were recorded in advance. "We hadn't decided which way to go with it," Diana recalls, "and I was sitting home by myself, listening to records, which I love to do. I put on Nat Cole's Love Letters, and then I listened to Julie London's Cry Me A River. I went through everything, Carmen McRae, everything. And I kept going back to Frank Sinatra. Songs like Maybe You'll Be There — I'd never heard him do that — Only The Lonely, Nice And Easy, You Go To My Head. The more I listened, the more I was blown away. God, I thought, how does Frank take lines from tunes like I Get Along Without You Very Well — 'Except perhaps in spring, but I should never think of spring' — rhyming 'spring' with 'spring' and make them work?"

Diana would gather an armful of albums and hustle over to LiPuma's Manhattan apartment. "We got onto the Sinatra thing very quickly," LiPuma says. "She pulled out SINATRA AT THE SANDS, which I hadn't heard, and I pulled some things she hadn't heard. And then Only The Lonely came on and we began to have a conscious beginning for the new album, not as a model, but as a direction for the songs." After making a basic selection of more than 30 possible choices, Diana and LiPuma reduced these choices to about 20 or so. Then the studio sessions began, some with Diana playing solo piano, some with small ensembles.

"The thing has gone through so many changes, from solo piano and voice, to trio and quartet tracks," Diana said later. "We did *The Night We Called It A Day* and *Cry Me A River* all in one day. And it was a great day. Everybody was having a groove day. And we did *Cry Me A River* on only the second take. We lived with them for a while, sort of allowing them to go through their own little growth process."

LiPuma remarks on one important consideration in their joint discussions of the content of the album. "You have a lot of different pressures that you're dealing with. You have an album that suddenly sells two million worldwide and obviously, the follow-up, there's a certain amount of pressure that you can't help but have. Everybody's watching. It would have been simple for us just to go back with the same winning team, to get Johnny. We're going to work with Johnny on her Christmas album, so it wasn't a question of her not liking what Johnny did. To the contrary. But we just wanted to do something a little different, instead of WHEN I LOOK IN YOUR EYES, VOLUME TWO." Diana herself agrees. "It's very different from my other albums," she says. "I felt as an artist, that's what I needed to do — whether it was going to sell records or not. So I've taken the risk to do something very, very different. To take on challenging lyrics, challenging pieces."

Some time around this point in their discussions, it had become clear to both LiPuma and Diana that the album would primarily be oriented toward ballads. They canceled a session that had been planned to record some lighter, up-tempo tunes to add the same kind of balance found in Diana's previous albums. Once this decision was made, the question arose of whether to proceed with the small ensemble format or to go for broke and take the more expensive and riskier route of involving Ogerman and bringing in an entire orchestra. Diana says that the decision for her was simple.

Ogerman and LiPuma were very old, even intimate friends. Ogerman had served as musical director in the early 1960s with Verve/MGM Records under Creed Taylor before LiPuma arrived. Together they produced the fabulously successful, BREEZIN', a Grammy-winning album by guitarist George Benson in 1979. A later album, called GATE OF DREAMS, based on highlights from Ogerman's ballet "Some Times," also produced by LiPuma, featured Ogerman's own orchestra with George Benson, David Sanborn, and Michael Brecker, followed by the CITYSCAPE album from GRP, and another album, CLAUS OGERMAN FEATURING MICHAEL BRECKER.

Ogerman's jazz credentials are indeed nothing short of awesome. Apart from his work with Michael Brecker, George Benson, and Bill Evans, he has also worked on Verve/MGM recordings by Wes Montgomery, Kai Winding, and Cal Tjader. He worked with Benny Goodman, Oscar Peterson, and Betty Carter, and wrote jazz charts for Stan Getz, Freddy Hubbard, and Stanley Turrentine. His best-known work is associated with the bossa nova creations of the likes of Astrud Gilberto and Joao Gilberto and Antonio Carlos Jobim, who gave Ogerman an entire side of his 1976 album URUBU to feature his strings. Jobim's 1980 album, TERRA BRASILIS, a reworking of his own arrangements from Jobim's 1960s American albums, also features Ogerman's piano-playing behind the trumpet stylings of Chet Baker, another favorite of Diana's.

Ogerman's work in the arena of popular music is also remarkable. His arrangements can be heard on best-selling albums by Connie Francis, the Drifters, and Leslie Gore. Since the 1970s Ogerman has devoted himself mainly to serious compositions, including a ballet score for the American Ballet Theater ("Some Times"), a work for jazz piano and orchestra for Bill Evans called SYMBIOSIS, a song cycle based on poems by Rabindranath Tagore recorded by Met soprano Judith Blegen and mezzo-soprano Brigitte Fassbaender, CONCERTO LIRICO AND SARABANDE-FANTASIE for violin and orchestra recorded by Aaron Rosand, 10 SONGS FOR CHORUS A-CAPELLA AFTER POEMS by Georg Heym recorded by the

Cologne Radio Chorus, and a work for violin and orchestra, PRE-LUDIO AND CHANT recorded by violinist Gideon Kremer.

Ogerman was at first reluctant to re-enter the world of popular music to work with Diana. He hadn't done a pure orchestration of anything other than his own classical writing in more than 22 years. But when Diana was in Munich and the opportunity arose, LiPuma organized a meeting between her and Ogerman. Over a five-hour dinner, Diana and Ogerman became happily acquainted as they talked about music and one of Diana's great loves, old movies. Diana's piano playing identity is said to have played a very important part in Ogerman's decision to join the project.

"You're getting into deep water when you do arrangements of songs Nelson Riddle has done," Ogerman says in regard to the LOOK OF LOVE project, "songs like *I Get Along Without You Very Well*, so you have to do it or you don't do it. And, in the 22 years I spent working on my classical pieces, I added a lot to my orchestral vocabulary, and I think the orchestrations I did for Diana reflect that fact." The orchestrations were recorded in late March when LiPuma and his trusted recording engineer, Al Schmitt, traveled to London to meet with Ogerman and the London Symphony Orchestra. In these studio sessions, Ogerman conducted his orchestral arrangements synchronously with the already recorded vocal tracks.

There were times when each of the participants was overcome with emotions hearing the results. "When we first heard *Only The Lonely*," Diana says, "Tommy wiped his eyes every time we came to the ending." (*Only The Lonely*, a classic tune previously performed by both Frank Sinatra and Roy Orbison, was not included on the final release.)

The finicky business of making sure that every element was in its proper place in the mix continued for some time. A week after the final mixing, LiPuma and his crew were back in the studio making adjustments. "You want it to be so perfect, and you get to the point where almost everything you try to adjust affects something else," he comments. LiPuma was torn in all kinds of different directions, as he told Don Heckman at the *Los Angeles Times*.

"Now I'm going through everything. Should *Cry Me A River* be cut No. 4? Should *Dancing In The Dark* be cut No. 6? Everything affects everything else. All of these things, particularly with the expectations surrounding this album, are important decisions. And here's where I have to think like an executive and take account of all the long-term marketing aspects of the album. Because this is an album that you want to have the effect of stopping people in their tracks." All the evidence suggests that Tony LiPuma has succeeded in his aims. Here is the sequence of tracks as he finally arranged them.

'S Wonderful is suddenly in the listener's ear, with a sweep of Ogerman's string and flute orchestrations and Diana's voice appearing as a subtle whisper surrounded by drums and guitar in the bossa nova style. Ella has done version upon version of this standard, also featuring strings, but after a sweetly sung introduction, her version takes on a jazzy, up-tempo feeling. Ella's voice and the instrumentation convey a feeling of free and easy elation, breaking out into openly brassy choruses, very different from Diana's restrained, even-toned reading of the song.

A lovely guitar introduction by Russell Malone precedes Diana's vocal entry to *Love Letters*, introducing a poetic narrative, this time of requited love, though the singer's lover is absent. Diana gives the song a quiet, thoughtful treatment, totally convincing. She sings for long moments unaccompanied, with the strings or guitar coming in behind her phrases, offering comment. The end of the vocal is followed by an extended coda of sweeping, deep-toned strings. Some commentators have remarked that these string passages are too lush, too dramatic, but if the listener allows these sounds to have their full effect, they serve to deepen the overall emotional effect of Diana's quiet vocals.

A long instrumental introduction with strings accompanying a quietly plucked guitar and a subtly dominating drum and cymbal beat in bossa-nova style on *I Remember You* is followed by Diana's quietly poetic vocal treatment of this song. She sounds happier here, but a mood of wistful memory fits the overall melancholy atmosphere of the album.

Diana's version of Arthur Hamilton's *Cry Me A River* echoes two of the greatest performers of this song, Ella Fitzgerald and Julie London. Russell Malone's guitar opens this tune in a bluesy style above a bed of strings, inducing a slightly ominous feeling. Diana's voice is husky, cool, slightly thrilling. Her voice is full of cool irony, vengeance, a touch of real scorn. The first chorus is followed by a sweetly plucked guitar break by Malone. Diana's intonations, timing, and phrasing are perfectly understated, drawing out the anger in the lyrics, but also introducing a note of icy humor but just enough warmth to suggest a continuing ambiguity in the relationship between the two lovers in the song. The once rejected woman now herself clearly rejects the new advances of the former lover, but holds out the possibility of a reconciliation — once the lover has actually cried a river of tears.

An Ella Fitzgerald version of this song features a bravura vocal as she demonstrates her singing chops, changing tempos and styles freely, introducing smooth vocal glissandos. From the outset, there is no possibility of reconciliation between the two lovers. She is satisfied to be telling her former lover off, dismissing him contemptuously. Her confident vocal treatment of the lyrics are the perfect expression of this attitude. The best-known version of this song was recorded by the seductive singer-actress Julie London in the late 1950s. She also leaves no possibility of reconciliation. Certain phrasings in Diana's version suggest that she has listened to both of these versions, borrowed some of their phrasings, but the borrowings are more like musical echoes, blended seamlessly into her own interpretation of the song.

Diana sings the Spanish song *Besame Mucho* in the softest possible tones at the bottom of her vocal register to create an atmosphere of slow, tropical passion, perhaps overly-lush, overly suggestive, as some critics have remarked. Diana's cool and liquid piano solo at the end undercuts the slow but heated mood of the rest of the song and engineers an insouciant departure.

Diana's lost, yearning presentation of *The Night We Called It A Day* undercuts the wit of the word play in the title. The character within the song is addressing either some close confidante or else musing aloud to herself, remembering the very moment of the end of a love affair. Diana's slow tempo phrasings bring out the poetry of the images.

> There was a moon out in space
> But a cloud drifted over its face
> You kissed me and went on your way
> The night we called it a day . . .
>
> The moon went down stars were gone
> But the sun didn't rise with the dawn
> There wasn't a thing left to say
> The night we called it a day
>
> There wasn't a thing left to say
> The night we called it a day
>
> — TOM ACKER / MATT DENNIS

A pretty piano solo contributes to the poetic, melancholic mood.

On the Howard Dietz and Arthur Schwartz son *Dancing In The Dark*, a long string introduction accompanied by a steady bossa nova percussion motif again introduces Diana's quiet vocal, emphasizing a sense of the loneliness of the lovers dancing together in the dark, "Looking for the light of a new love to brighten up the night." Diana's repetition of the words "dancing in the dark" enhances a feeling of darkness, uncertainty, almost of menace and terror, and so does the dark oceanic sound of Claus Ogerman's string arrangement.

Diana's rendering of Hoagy Carmichael's *I Get Along Without You Very Well* is quiet, slow, regretful. The little drama contained in the song outlines a chance encounter between two former lovers. Most singers treat the lyrics so as to suggest a kind of false bravado on the part of the rejected lover, dramatically overturned by the final words of the song, which finds the singer brokenhearted.

... I get along without you very well
Of course I do
Except perhaps in spring
But I should never think of spring
For that would surely break my heart in two

    — HOAGY CARMICHAEL

When Diana sings, "I've forgotten you, just like I should," she introduces a touching note of falsely bright optimism — the singer is being brave. Her rendering of the lines suggests a wistful mood, rather than a plea for sympathy — "Please come back to me, because I'm so brave and sad." By a curious reversal, the abandoned lover seems to be doing all right, making the sudden change of mood expressed in the final words seem all the more acute.

A limpid piano solo follows Diana's equally limpid vocal treatment of the opening chorus of the Burt Bacharach and Hal David pop classic, *The Look of Love*. While this is unquestionably the most hopeful song on an album of mostly very sad songs, Diana's voice is almost heartbreaking in yearning for love as she renders the lines, "I can't wait to put my arms around you, how long I have waited," and in her repetition of the words, "Don't ever go, don't ever go." Diana performs this song to the limits of her considerable acting abilities, without ever stepping over the line into histrionics.

After a few deep-toned chords from the strings, to establish a mood of deep melancholy, the orchestra drops out momentarily, leaving Diana and the rhythm section alone to carry the first verse of *Maybe You'll Be There*.

Each time I see a crowd of people
Just like a fool I stop and stare
It's really not the proper thing to do
But maybe you'll be there ...

    — RUBE BLOOM / SAMMY GALLOP

Russell Malone contributes a particularly beautiful and haunting solo instrumental break between two later verses, accompanied lightly by strings.

If obsessing over lost love is a kind of neurosis, this is surely the most neurotic song on the album, in fact in all of Diana's work. It speaks of a kind of deep emotional dependency, a debilitating melancholy, extreme sadness.

> ... Someday if all my prayers are answered
> I'll hear a footstep on the stair
> With anxious heart
> I'll hurry to the door
> And maybe you'll
> Be there

While the THE LOOK OF LOVE has enjoyed unparalleled commercial success, some critics have found the album overwhelmingly sad in mood and excessively slow in tempo, self-indulgent and soporific. Diana's tempos on this album are often slow; ballads that others have sung slowly, Diana sings even more slowly, creating a lulling effect. This effect seems deliberate, though, for the songs are presented as lullabies, intended to provide consolation in a world that is overcharged and moving fast. Most popular music today achieves its effects by increasing speed and volume. Not so with Diana Krall. Her music creates a quiet place where the deepest emotions can be entertained, however painfully. More than any other singer today, Diana Krall allows for sadness. Some may call it self-indulgence, but the music she sings provides a space for healing, where these 'tough' emotions can be released.

Diana herself is aware that many of the songs recorded on THE LOOK OF LOVE are almost too sad. After hearing her own voice with Claus Ogerman's strings for the first time on *I Get Along Without You Very Well*, Diana confesses that "I listened to it and I just fell apart." Outside the studio, away from the group of principals listening to the recording, she had a good cry until Tommy

LiPuma came outside to offer her consolation. "A lot of this album was very sad," Diana notes, "and we had to go, 'people are not going to be ... (she breaks off) ... you're going to have to put a little razor blade and a Prozac in there, and a ticket to the pub — two drinks free'."

Afterword:
The Jazz **P**olice

The remarkable commercial success of Diana Krall's THE LOOK OF LOVE, following in the wake of her highly-publicized Grammy victory for vocal performance on WHEN I LOOK IN YOUR EYES, was accompanied by an outright explosion of critical controversy. All the old issues surrounding Diana's success surfaced again and boiled over in the press. The question, "Has Diana Krall gone pop?" as was posed in the title of an article by Toronto *Globe and Mail* critic Mark Miller, became the focus of contention. "Some jazz critics question her seriousness as a jazz artist when she seems to wander into the popular jazz vocalist category," another critic wrote.

Indeed, some 'jazz' critics, as distinct from 'popular music' critics, were outrightly hostile toward the record. Other less bellicose critics expressed regret that Diana's piano-playing had fallen into the background in the new album, swamped, in their opinion, by a heavy overload of Claus Ogerman's string accompaniments. In *PopMatters*, John Kreicbergs wrote, "Krall's piano work is practically non-existent on most of the tracks, save for a few perfunctory solos that often sink into a sea of overly lush string and orchestral arrangements. ... Instead of a group effort, the bulk of the work becomes a competition between Krall's vocals and Claus

Ogerman's orchestral arrangements. Krall's voice is shoved to the front of the mix, forcing the listener to examine every breath inhalation and phrase-ending consonant." The "sway and swell" of Ogerman's string arrangements, Kreicberg adds, "at times border on relegating the tunes to a Disneyesque feel."

Ken Dryden, in the *All Music Guide*, avers that "this somewhat ridiculously packaged Verve CD seems like an obvious attempt to turn her into a pop icon, and sex symbol to boot. The bland arrangements by Claus Ogerman . . . border on easy listening, while Krall and her various supporting musicians, including John Pisano, Russell Malone, Christian McBride, and Peter Irskine (among others), clearly seem stifled by their respective roles." Striking at the image of Diana projected in the album package, Dryden continues, "What is even sillier is the label's insistence on attempting to photograph the artist in various sultry poses."

Too pop, too sultry to be a bona fide jazz artist — these are the charges Diana Krall has faced from critics she calls the "Jazz Police," an allusion to Leonard Cohen's song of this title.

> ... Jazz police are looking through my folders
> Jazz police are talking to my niece
> Jazz police have got their final orders
> Jazzer, drop your axe, it's Jazz police!
>
> — LEONARD COHEN

Diana Krall's public image is a thorny question. To the critics who suggest that the glamorous photographs on her albums are a cheap attempt on the part of her managers to capitalize on her sex appeal, to turn her into a sex-symbol at the expense of musical values, to make her into a pop mannequin for the sake of the market, Diana has replied, "Yeah, but the core of that machinery is myself. So that's what is the most important thing, that I am in control of my own life. It's not they, them, the machine, marketing, blahblahblah, that is pushing me. It's these people working together." To which she adds, "I have such good people around me, in every aspect of my life. There's an abundance of support, safety nets, encouragement, no bullshit. There are people who look me directly in the eye and tell me exactly what they think, regardless of what I say, and know that I respect their opinion and also know that they don't have to go, 'Oh, we cannot tell her what to do.' "

Following her years working with Mary Ann Topper and the Jazz Tree in the early 1990s, Diana changed managers in 1998, moving to S.L. Feldman & Associates, a Vancouver based company who also manage Joni Mitchell, the Canadian-born singer-songwriter who has traversed an entire range of musical styles from folk and rock through pop and jazz. While Mary Ann Topper has no clear idea why Diana left her firm, she holds no ill will. Perhaps Diana was attracted to the idea of working with a Canadian company, close to home. Perhaps she wanted to break away from the grueling tour schedule Jazz Tree had set for her in small clubs and at low-paying jazz festivals, as her friend John Capon suggests. Perhaps she saw an opportunity to grow musically and financially. Kerry Gold in the *Vancouver Sun* reports that Diana first approached Steve Macklam, a partner in Sam Feldman's operation, at a Juno awards party in Vancouver to discuss the possibility of working with him to expand the horizons of her jazz market by negotiating a cross-over campaign into the larger arena of pop music. Macklam's success in managing the transition of The Chieftains from their traditional Celtic folk audience to a wider pop-based market was well known. Drawing on this crossover experience, Macklam developed a new promotional plan for Diana Krall. Diana was pleased. "Joni Mitchell, The Chieftains. These aren't flash-in-the-pan pop people. They're artists who have seen a lot and they've put their trust in Steve and Sam."

The management philosophy of S.L. Feldman & Associates and the strategy used to promote Diana Krall was profiled as a business story in the Financial Post section of the *National Post*, the Canadian equivalent to the *Wall Street Journal*. As journalist David Hayes defines the decisive role of a personal manager in the promotion of any recording artist, "Personal managers can be considered both the CEO and the COO of an artist's business. They are involved in day-to-day career development and personal guidance, as well as planning a long-range strategy for an artist's career. While a record company is focussed solely on maximizing revenue potential for the CDs released under the terms of an artist's contract, managers co-ordinate every aspect of an artist's business. Along with trying to ensure that clients are made a priority at their record companies, managers work with booking agents to make sure tours run smoothly and profitably, negotiate sponsorships and field overtures from media, charities and other parties." In describing management styles beyond the stereotype of a Svengali, Hayes notes, "Among big-time managers, some are abrasive bullies; others, like Macklam and Feldman, are smooth and unflappable." And some managers, like Steve Macklam, have a special "knack for taking the ephemeral qualities of artists, and by exploiting opportunities, transforming them into successful commodities without endangering the artist's image."

Sam Feldman and Steve Macklam have earned a reputation as managers who place the interests of the artists in first place. Joni Mitchell is notorious for the commercial risks she has taken while following her artistic path from folk to pop to jazz singer. "Macklam and Feldman," David Hayes remarks, "have no desire to control their artists. Rather, their philosophy is to work with clients who have strong artistic visions. In the case of Krall, their role — for 15% of gross earnings — is to help position her further into the mainstream, giving her a durable career that exploits global markets and gains additional support from carefully considered corporate partnerships, while ensuring that she doesn't lose her jazz bona fides."

The challenges of promoting a jazz act, as opposed to a pop act, are considerable, as Macklam explains. "This is a jazz project. It doesn't follow the same formulae as pop music. We don't have at our disposal all the conventional tools: the hit records, the MTV-style video airplay. We don't have much point-of-purchase advertising, either, because the retail space available to jazz artists isn't normally very large. So it leaves you with two traditional tools: performance and press. Which means that Diana's international success depends even more upon management."

Good managers recognize that musicians, like athletes, have "career arcs when they're as successful as they're going to be," Macklam believes. "It's the role of management to make as much money as possible during that peak without compromising the artist's integrity." A good manager builds the momentum an artist needs to reach the apex of the arc, while widening the audience base for the long term. Macklam's efforts on behalf of Diana Krall have been directed towards developing both a fresh, new audience and a long-lasting fan base for her. He had accomplished this with The Chieftains, by working smaller, but nonetheless important markets to achieve a critical mass of fan support. The Chieftains were booked, not only into the main cities of the Canadian market — Toronto, Montreal and Vancouver — but also into other second-tier cities like Edmonton, Saskatoon, and Victoria, then into small international venues, before tackling the American market. With Diana, this same approach has been used. Before the release of THE LOOK OF LOVE, Macklam had booked Diana for concert appearances in first and second-tier cities in Canada, France, Britain, Germany, Spain, and Southeast Asia. All of these concerts sold out, in part on account of Macklam's hard work in arranging press interviews, corporate sponsorships, and television appearances in major cities throughout the world. Because of this work, Diana has charted number one hits in Singapore, Kuala Lumpur, and Portugal, a number three record in Mexico, and a number seven hit in France.

Part of Steve Macklam's task has been to lobby the executives of Verve to expend as much as possible of the company's resources to promote Diana's career, consulting at every step in recent years with Tommy LiPuma and with subsidiaries of Verve in Europe. He has convinced Daniel Richard, who runs Verve in France, to release a substantial amount of his advertising budget to promote Diana's records and appearances there. He has also been successful in landing important corporate sponsorships for Diana in ad campaigns for Eaton's, Rolex, and Daimler-Chrysler

Canada. And Macklam has cracked the point-of-purchase barrier by placing 250,000 copies of THE LOOK OF LOVE in Target, the American department store chain. Appearances by Diana on the Conan O'Brien, David Letterman, and Larry King shows were engineered by his enterprise, in preparation for a two-month long tour of concert venues in the United States during spring 2002.

There is no doubt that the image of Diana Krall promoted by S.L. Feldman & Associates has tremendous public appeal, fully recognized and appropriated by Pearl Davies, the brand manager for Daimler-Chrysler, as reported in the *National Post*. "You can say she epitomizes the core essence of the Chrysler brand," Davies explains. "We talk about four things: expressive, refined, athletic and romantic. When we talk about expressive, we mean self-evident beauty of vehicles. You could call them drop dead gorgeous. When you look at Diana you don't need to say another thing about that. Then we talk about the refinement of the vehicles, the quality of the craftsmanship, and we can draw a parallel between her art and our vehicles. When we talk about athleticism, we mean performance and grace. When Diana performs, and everything about her, it suggests graceful poise. And this year we've added the concept of romantic. That's about passion, building cars for people to fall in love with. What better way to express it than with Diana Krall, who sings about love, the look of love, let's fall in love . . ." Strip away the sales pitch and this becomes an evocation of the appeal not only of Diana Krall's image, but also her music — a perfect fit of art and image. Music is, after all, a performance art. And love — the language of love, in words and images — is the focus of Diana Krall's musical enterprise and perhaps the source of her commercial appeal.

The word 'love' itself or a direct allusion to love is included in almost all the titles to the songs she sings, in all her album titles. Her career as a singer has been an exploration of the nuances of the emotions associated with love, from melancholy to joy, from romance to irony, from hurting to healing, from desire fulfilled to desire frustrated. While there is nothing novel in making love the subject of music — love songs are as old as human history —

Diana's approach to this age-old subject is remarkable for being so diverse and so — dare we say it — appealing. Diana Krall's genius has been to bring her commercial appeal to the service of her art, rather than music to the service of commerce. "Everybody has to do some sort of marketing in their life," Diana has observed. "Tommy LiPuma says, 'You know, you make a beautiful record, you make the record. Then those guys over there, in that department, they market it.' My job is to keep the music honest."

The marketing executives at Verve have stated that Diana Krall has become the Elvis Presley of the label, meaning that her commercial success is now enabling the production of albums by other emerging artists. Diana Krall is contributing to the development of the jazz, while at the same time bringing a new audience to the jazz tradition, however 'unsophisticated' the jazz police may find these fans.

Diana has always seemed to possess the uncanny ability to make it clear that behind the dramatic act, behind the pose, behind the image, there is a real person dwelling with real feelings. If the image conceals as much as it reveals, it does so in order that the real personality behind the image may remain not so much invulnerable as intact, because the real person has too much vulnerability, too much human concern. Unlike the case of Madonna, where we see the apotheosis of self-love and naked personal ambition, what exists in Diana Krall is the expansion of the personality so as to make room for growth in the music and its expressive power.

No, Verve Records and S.L. Feldman & Associates have not distorted Diana Krall to exploit the market. They have presented her as she chooses to be presented, which is true to her character as a performer, as anyone can see who traces her image from STEPPING OUT to THE LOOK OF LOVE. Diana Krall is consistent, which suggests she is genuine. And according to Diana, Steve Macklam and Sam Feldman have never crossed the artistic line, directing what she should record to exploit a market. "Sometimes I've been agonizing over decisions," Diana notes, "and I'll say, 'You have to help me with this.' They would say, 'We're going to manage you and help make happen what you want to happen.' But they've had the courage and strength to say, 'You're just going to have to figure it out for yourself.' With some artistic decisions, it's been challenging, but I'm better for it and they've always been there for me. I'm very thankful for them. I'm very thankful."

If Diana Krall is not guilty as charged by the jazz police for using sultry photographs to sell jazz records to unsuspecting pop fans, she has still had to defend herself against the charge of selling her jazz soul to pop devils. In the September 25 edition of the *Village Voice*, Gary Giddins gave a strange political spin to his criticism of Diana Krall, comparing her performance on THE LOOK OF LOVE to the post September 11 "flat mannerisms" of American President George W. Bush. "Similarly, Krall, who was so imaginative and even lively in her recent concert appearances and on last year's WHEN I LOOK IN YOUR EYES, has knuckled to flat mannerisms on THE LOOK OF LOVE (Verve), an intermittently pleasing lite-jazz set orchestrated by veteran menace Claus Ogerman, who, lacking the honest schmaltz of a Gordon Jenkins, resorts instead to drawn-out endings and showy classical lifts. Deprived of her cheery trio, Krall is reduced to decorative piano solos ('Love Letters'), Joao Gilberto and Julie London imitations, half-spoken phrases, and practiced groans. She is better than this, better than lite, better than Ogerman, better than the booklet's cheesecake."

If Giddins found some strange similarity between the orchestrated performances of George W. Bush and Diana's Krall's new album, Stephen Holden in the *New York Times* found an equally strange political solace in her music. "Over an insinuating bossa nova beat Claus Ogerman's ominously beautiful arrangement for Diana Krall's *Dancing In The Dark* rolls in like overlapping waves on a rising tide ahead of an approaching coastal storm. . . . That recording, with its balance of beauty and terror, became a personal touchstone to which I returned again and again in the wake of the events of September 11. The lyric's uncertainty and fatalism voiced a commonly felt mood of despair: the fearful intimation that even if there was a future it still might be too bleak to contemplate." It's hard to know whether Diana might have been inclined to burn or frame this remark, which casts her in the role of a kind of jazz/pop prophetess, in the light of the fact that THE LOOK OF LOVE was in preparation long before the tragic events of September 11, and it seems highly unlikely that the immediate commercial success of the album was in any way related to these tragic events, retrospectively or otherwise. In fact, Diana canceled a launch of the album scheduled at Toronto's Union Station in respect for the victims of the terrorist attacks and spent the day of the record's release walking around New York City with her boyfriend as a way of commemorating the victims and their families.

Between these poles of denigration and idolization other critics looked for a common ground. In his otherwise friendly review, *Washington Post* staff writer Michael Dirda remarked that the album was "overorchestrated in places and almost too sorrowful," then introduced the debate over whether Diana's music was jazz or pop. "You might call her a lounge singer-pianist, but only if you think of *Moby Dick* as merely a long book about a whale." In the *Globe and Mail*, Heather Mallick quotes *"Down Beat's* critic emeritus," John McDonough, as saying, "It's a lovely album. But I don't think of it as a jazz album any more than I would consider Linda Ronstadt's trilogy of Nelson Riddle to be jazz albums." Adding his opinion that the orchestral arrangements and the singing on THE LOOK OF LOVE are both wonderful, McDonough believes Diana remains an artist who can perform credibly with a jazz combo and who can return to jazz any time she wants. "I don't think being popular is necessarily to lower yourself," he continues. "In rating it, I would certainly rate it four stars." Nevertheless, he remains adamant, "But it's not a jazz album."

In response to this kind of criticism, Diana has responded, "I had a poster of Peter Frampton and a poster of Charlie Parker in my room when I was a teenager. But for you jazz police out there, don't worry — I arranged them so they couldn't see each other." She also responded to a charge laid by Tony Moon in the *Houston Chronicle* that her music not only "deflects attention from the more substantial contributions of Shirley Horn, Cassandra

Wilson and others, it confirms the prevailing wisdom that new jazz CD's are simply lifestyle enhancers — a little schmaltz, a hint of silky audio glamor to complement the fine chardonnay." To which Diana replied, "It's not my place to apologize or say I'm overrated because there are a lot of other great singers. There are certainly great singers out there and I hope people support the art form more. It's not my responsibility to bring jazz to the audience, but if I talk about Diana Reeves or Cassandra Wilson and other great jazz singers, maybe people will start buying it."

An unnamed critic from *Jazzitude* attempts to resolve the debate with this sensible remark: "The bottom line is that it is wonderful and amazing that an artist of Krall's stature has caught the ear of the record-buying public. Some will see her in concert and no doubt be amazed at her abilities as a pianist, a few might even become life-long listeners of jazz as a result of their exposure to Diana Krall. And she is definitely a fine singer and interpreter of torch songs — in my opinion, she is truly what Frank Sinatra called (defining himself) 'a saloon singer'." The overwhelming fact was that few listeners cared one way or another what label was fitted on Diana's vocal artistry.

Down Beat critic Josef Woodward calls Diana the "Chairwoman of the Board," echoing Frank Sinatra's title as Chairman of the Board. "Once every generation an artist comes along who transcends a particular style of music and broadens its audience to the masses. For modern jazz music, that artist is undoubtedly Diana Krall." As he points up, "What's with kids these days — favoring Sinatra-esqueries over Radiohead? Therein lies part of Krall's all-important function in musical culture at the moment: She brings together listeners from wildly diverse age and cultural demographics. In a divisive age, she unites, whether she cares to admit it or not." *New York Times* jazz critic Peter Watrous comes to a similar conclusion about the pop appeal of Diana Krall's jazz. "She's making really, really beautiful acoustic music which people can *like*," he emphasizes. "I think that one of the great sort of challenges of American art in the twentieth century has been how to balance the popular impulse with something good. And obviously the great figures have done it, whether it's Charlie Chaplin, Ernest Hemingway, or Duke Ellington. And I think that she's come up with a balance that really works. People like what she does, and it's in no way an adolescent sellout — it's something smart, sophisticated, and good."

As early as 1996, Diana Krall declared her intention to reach across the divide between jazz and pop music. "I've played pop stuff in piano bars, and I wouldn't mind singing on a pop record or a commercial. I'm game, but playing the music I *want* to play is the most important thing. I grew up with eclectic tastes at home musically, but my heart is in the *groove*. I just want to play piano and sing. The bottom line is the music, the music, the *music!*" Elsewhere she has stated, "I went into music because I love music and I was hoping to get a gig. Now I'm kind of popular, so I'm getting asked questions whether or not I'm going to become pop . . . I'm so busy touring and working, that right now, I'm just worried about playing. The music is more important than anything else." In the same breath, she acknowledges a difference between her storytelling approach to her singing and her swinging jazz approach to the piano: "I look at myself more as a storyteller kind of singer rather than a jazz singer. . . . The lyric is really important for me. It has to be very strong and timeless. . . . I'm approaching the piano definitely as a jazz player, and that's where I do the improvising." Diana closes her defence of all charges by the jazz police, neatly. "I think right now I'm doing the best work I can be doing at this stage in my life. If the jazz police don't like it, I don't give a damn."

If Diana suffered any hurt feelings on account of some of the harsh criticism she has received, it has been amply assuaged by friendly comments from musical colleagues across the music spectrum. When she met Quincy Jones backstage on the Conan O'Brien television show, the reigning king of producers congratulated her. As she tells the story, "He walked up to me and said, 'Diana, Claus Ogerman, the London Symphony Orchestra, and entering No. 9 in the pop charts and No. 1 in Canada! This is great for music!'" Elton John, a pop idol of the young Diana, met her in Hawaii shortly after the announcement of her Grammy nomination for WHEN I LOOK IN YOUR EYES. They became fast friends. The next time they met, Sir Elton arrived carrying all of her CDs, asking for autographs. "Diana is a very gifted pianist," Elton John has remarked, "but if it's vocals you're talking about . . . Okay, she's not a scat jazzer in the way that Ella was. Instead, she uses her voice very sparingly and beautifully in the way that Peggy Lee or June Christy did. But that doesn't make her any less amazing. For a start, she absolutely has her own style, which is the hardest thing in the world for any of us to achieve. And as for that level of insight and sophistication — just amazing. She takes a song that you've heard a thousand other singers do a million times before, and it's as if you're hearing it for the first time. And understanding it properly, too. I have not one doubt that she's a legend of the future. Absolutely, she is around to stay."

Elton John hints at the secret of Diana Krall's appeal as an artist. There is indeed something unique about her music. While there are at least a dozen popular singers active today who have better voices than Diana Krall in terms of range and volume — Aretha Franklin, Whitney Houston, Celine Dion, Barbra Streisand, Annie Lennox, Etta James, Dionne Warwick, Bette Midler, Mariah Carey, Natalie Cole, Trisha Yearwood, and Faith Hill, to name a few — none have her sense of 'cool'. Diana Krall is a singer like Billie Holiday, Patsy Cline, or Edith Piaf. Limited in her vocal range and power, Diana must rely on other musical qualities — tempo, silence, and nuance. Unable to use bold vocal effects, Diana Krall has become a conversational singer who exploits the 'weaknesses' in her own voice — the thin and occasionally gravely tone — to evoke emotional effects which usually disappear in the sublime dramatic perfection and purity of the operatic voice.

Whitney Houston may astonish us with a dozen vocal feats in a single song, but Diana cannot do this. She must rely instead on the subtlety of her interpretation of the song, using her conversational intonation and storytelling charm to convey the emotional center of the song she has fully inhabited. While other voices invite us to admire the vocal performance, Diana Krall's voice implicates, it insinuates, it whispers, it seduces, and it invites the listener to join her in the fantasy, the inner drama of the song, to become an actor as much as a listener. Diana Krall's music invites us to play a role in the drama of love.

Diana Krall's art is minimalist, the art of the restrained and understated phrase and gesture. Feelings are intensified by this simplicity. Undemanding on the surface, Diana's songs always contain hidden depths. To use that term introduced into our musical vocabulary by saxophone saint Lester Young and popularized with the release of Miles Davis' album BIRTH OF THE COOL, Diana Krall's music is not hot or loud, not cold and refined, not warm or mellow — Diana Krall's music is cool.

References

Books

Anderson, Christopher. *Madonna.* New York: Island Books, 1991.

Brown, Jim. *Country Women in Music.* Kingston, ON: Quarry Music Books, 1999.

Clooney, Rosemary, with Barthel, Jean. *Girl Singer, An Autobiography.* New York: Doubleday, 1999.

Crouse, Richard. *The Celine Dion Story: A Voice and a Dream.* New York: Ballantyne Books, 1998.

Dickerson, James. *Women On Top: The Quiet Revolution That's Rocking the American Music Industry.* New York: Billboard Books, 1998.

Gourse, Leslie *Unforgettable: The Life and Mystique of Nat King Cole.* New York: St. Martin's Press, 1991.

Gray, Scott. *The Shania Twain Story: On Her Way.* New York: Ballantyne Books, 1998.

Miller, Mark. *The Miller Companion to Jazz in Canada and Canadians in Jazz.* Toronto: The Mercury Press, 2001.

Norcross, E. Blanche. *Nanaimo Retrospective: The First Century.* Nanaimo: Nanaimo Historical Society, 1979.

Rosenthal, David H. *Hard Bop*. New York: Oxford University Press, 1992.

Ward, Geoffrey C., and Burns, Ken. *Jazz: A History of America's Music*. New York: Alfred K. Knopf, 2000.

Starr, Victoria, *k.d. lang: All You Get Is Me*. Toronto: Random House of Canada, 1994.

Woodworth, Marc and Hanson, Emma Dodge. *Solo*. New York: Dell Publishing Group, 1998.

Periodicals

Alexiou, Dimetre. "Playing it Cool—Diana Krall at the Trump Marina," *The Gambler Magazine*, January 9, 2002.

Andrews, Marke. "Diana—Her True Story, from Small-town Girl to New York Chanteuse, and all that Jazz," *The Vancouver Sun*, March 7, 1995.

Andrews, Marke. "Krall Hits the Sweet Spot," *Vancouver Sun*, June 6, 1999.

Anonymous. "Diana Krall: Songs of Love," *USA Today*, Music, September 5, 1999.

Anonymous. "Krall Adds Orchestral Passages to New Release," *Vancouver Sun*, April 30, 2001.

Anonymous. "Krall Stories," *Arts & Entertainment*, December 8, 2001.

Anonymous. "Nanaimo Singer Newest U.S. Songbird," *Nanaimo Daily Free Press*, February 2, 1995.

Bourne, Michael. "For the Fun of It," *Down Beat*, July 1996.

Chamberlain, Adrian. "Nanaimo's Golden Girl of Jazz," *Victoria Times-Colonist*, February 14, 1998, c7.

Chapman, Geoff. "B.C. Inspired Love Scenes," *Vancouver Province*, November 13, 1997.

Edelstein, Paula. "Diana Krall Sings a Subtle Song," *AAJ General Article*, June, 1999.

Fordham, John. "Is That All There Is? No Not Really," *Guardian*, December 4, 1999.

Hayes, David. "The Boys in the Brand," *National Post*, February 27, 2002.

Gill, Alexandra. "The Making of Diana Krall," *The Globe and Mail*, October 13, 2001.

Gold, Kerry. "The Jazz Singer: Diana Krall," *Vancouver Sun*, March 31, 2001, A1, A16.

Gold, Kerry. "Love for Music, Krall Style," *Vancouver Sun*, March 31, 2000.

Goldman, Vivien. "Diana Krall and Tony Bennett," *Interview*, August, 2000.

Heckman, Don. "Krall Crafts Follow-up to Hit Album," *Vancouver Sun*, April 30, 2001; rpt. from *Los Angeles Times*.

Jennings, Nicholas. "Diana Krall," *Maclean's*, September 13, 1999, 45.

Kerr, Alison. "The Jazz Singer," *The Herald Magazine*, September 18, 2001.

King, Bill. "Interview with Diana Krall," *Jazz Report*, n.d.

Lekich, John. "Krall Mixes Style with Substance," *Georgia Straight*, June 11-18, 1998.

Massarik, John. "Diana, Queen of Jazz," *Evening Standard* (London), July 3, 2001.

Miller, Mark. "Diana Krall's Long Haul," *Globe and Mail*, November, 1997.

Nazareth, Errol. "A Cool Warm Chat," *Toronto Sun*, January 14, 1999.

Pielou, Adrianne. "Diana, Doddess of Jazz," *You*, n.d.

Quill, Greg. "Diana Krall in the Spotlight," *Toronto Star*; rpt. *Vancouver Sun*, January 14, 2000.

Ratliff, Ben. "Jazz Latte," *New York Times Magazine*, February 20, 2000.

Rosens, Aleksandrs. "Feature: Diana Krall Swings Her Way to the Grammys Again," *Reuters*, February 4, 2000.

Santisi, Ray. "Recollections of Diana," *Berklee Today*, Fall 1999.

Stevenson, Jane. "Krall Cool to Controversy," *Toronto Sun*, October 24, 2001.

Shadwick, Keith. "Di's the Limit," *Jazzwise*, September, 2001.

Stevenson, Jane. "Jazzing up the Grammys," *Toronto Sun*, February 20, 2000.

Thigpen, David E. "And She Swings, TOO," *Time*, June, 1996.

Tye, Dana. "Singing Success," *Nanaimo Times*, June 24, 1993.

Weddle, Eric. "Giving the Drummer Some," *Bloomington Independent*. n.d.

Wells, Paul. "White Girls Can Sing," *Saturday Night*, September, 1996.

Woodard, Josef. "Chairwoman of the Board," *Down Beat*, September 2001.

Internet Sites

http://findarticles.com/cf_iview/ml285/8_30/645666615/pl/article.jhtml

http://www.canoe.ca/JamMusicArtistsB/bennett_tony.html

http://www.canoe.ca/JamMusicArtistsK/krall_diana.html

http://www.hopper-management.com/dk_bio_e.htm

Jean-Michel Reisser, "And Diana arrived," quoted in full in "The Look of Love," CD review Louis Gerber, http://www.cosmopolis.ch/english/cosmo19/diana_krall.htm

http://www.lajazzsociety.org/LAIS/Programs/Tribute/Past/Jimmyu%20Rowles.htm

http://www.pbs.org/jazz/biography/artist_id_rowles_jimmy.htm and

http://music.barnesandnoble.com/search/artistbio.asp?

userId=&mscssid=&pCount=&sRefer. . .

Carol Sloane, "The First Time I Saw Jimmy Rowles,"

http://www.allaboutjazz.com/articles/ftiso300.htm

http://www.johnclaytonjazz.com/about_john/main/index.html

http://hopper-management.com/jc_bio_e.htm

http://www.hamiltonjazz.com/hamiltonbio.html

http://indepen.com/2001/Nov01.01/music6.html

http://www.justin-time.com/news/?JservSessionldneur06=89i4qgvr51

http://www.justin-time.com/label/

http://www.vervemusicgroup.com/grp/top.html

http://www.nprjazz.org/programs/sturrentine.atc.html

http://members.tripod.com/~hardbop/stanley.html

http://www.jazzradio.org/christia.htm

http://www.thepeaches.com/music/composers/kern/FolksWho-
LiveOnTheHill.txt

http://www.nat-king-cole.org/oldpages/milestones.htm

http://amazon.com/exec/obidos/tg/feature/-/202266/ref=ed_
ec_h_cs_14_3/026-71179

http://www.fortunecity.com/tinpan/newbonham/6/frimfram.htm

"Verve/GRP Producer Tommy LiPuma on the making of *When I Look in
Your Eyes*,"

http://www.berklee.edu/bt/112/k.lipuma.html

http://digitalinterviews.com/digitalinterviews/views/mcbride.shtml

http://www.delafont.com/music-acts/diana-krall.htm

Pieter Hoffman, "Diana Krall—chanteuse,"
http://www.fly.co.uk/diana.html

http://www.npr.org/programs/jazzprofiles/jmandel.html

http:www.therecord.com/entertainment/entertainment_011018103020
.html

http:www.sessions54.com/artists/krall03/

http//www.allaboutjazz.com/articles/a0699_02.htm

http:www.sessions54.com/artists/krall03/

http://www.bjbear71.com/Ogerman/Claus-3.html, but this site credits
the information

[from Robert Farnon society (incl. Percy Faith) at http://www.rfsoc.
freeserve.co.uk]

http//www.usatoday.com/life/music/lmds647.htm

http://www.berklee.edu/bt/112/k.recollections.html

http://www.thegamblermagazine.com/gamblermagazine/pub/article as
p?

section=1&article

http://www.rosemaryclooney.com/krall.html

http://www.shm.com.au/news/0112/08/entertainment/entertain7.html

www.jazzreport.com/interviews/diana-krall.html)

http:/www.canoe.ca/JamMusicArtistsK/krall_diana.html

http://www.canoe.ca/JamMusicArtistsK/krall_diana.html

Acknowledgements

Without the support, love, encouragement, and assistance of my wife, Carol, this book would never have been possible. Many thanks to my editor, Bob Hilderley, for his strong editorial assistance in pulling the manuscript together at the end. Thanks to all my friends for their support and encouragement. And my warmest thanks to all of the people below for important contributions to this book:

Jim Brown, Janice Buie and the staff at the Vancouver Island Reference Library, John Capon, Renee Doruyter, S.L. Feldman and Associates and staff, Ross Fraser, Gary Gaudet, Evelyn and Burt Hepinstall, Joyce Horner, Steve Jones, Lorrie Kean, Rick Kilburn, Tim Lander, David Levinson at S.L. Feldman & Associates, Scott Littlejohn, Gail Manz, Linda Martin, Carol Matthews, Mike Matthews, John Orysik and Ken Pickering of the Coastal Jazz and Blues Society, Neil Ritchie ("Hot Air," CBC Vancouver), Louise Rose, Joani Taylor, Sandra Thomson and the staff at the Port Theatre in Nanaimo, Mary Ann Topper, Bob Turner, Ron Smith, Bryan Stovell, Gavin Walker, Bruce Williams and the staff at New VITV, Nanaimo, Jim West and Arlene Cohen of Justin Time Records.

Photo Credits